The Winter Whale

The Winter Whale

Jim Crumley

BIRLINN

First published in 2008 by
Birlinn Limited
West Newington House
10 Newington Road
Edinburgh
EH9 1QS

www.birlinn.co.uk

ISBN13: 978 1 84158 732 5
ISBN10: 1 84158 732 X

British Library Cataloguing-in-Publication Data
A catalogue record for this book is available from the British Library

Design and typeset by Iolaire Typesetting, Newtonmore
Printed and bound by CPI Cox & Wyman, Reading, RG1 8EX

Remember well

JEAN GARSON
(1928–2008)

Contents

Acknowledgements

I owe my greatest debt of thanks to the staff of the local history section of Dundee's Wellgate Library for unearthing the bones of the story in a small mountain of 125-year-old newspaper cuttings. Their knowledge and patience simply made this book possible, and reaffirmed my belief that libraries are treasures beyond price and it is therefore impossible to over-invest in them.

I should also express my gratitude to the shades of those anonymous hacks who had such fun with the story of the Tay Whale in the columns of the two Dundee newspapers of the day, the *Advertiser* and the *Courier,* and to D.C. Thomson, Dundee-based publishers of newspapers of distinction to this very day.

My thanks are also due to a number of publishers for permission to quote from their titles. First among these is *Among Whales* (Scribner, 1998) by Roger Payne. The world of whale biology has no more eloquent ambassador than Roger Payne. *Among Whales* is not just a scientist's passionate exposition of his chosen field of endeavour. It is, remarkably among the written works of biologists, an accomplished work of literature to stand alongside the best nature writers of the twentieth century. Special mention is also appropriate for Norman Watson's well-crafted and impressively researched book, *The Dundee Whalers* (Tuckwell, 2003).

Thanks also to the publishers of Heathcote Williams's extraordinary long poem *Whale Nation* (Cape, 1988), Farley Mowat's *A Whale for the Killing* (McLelland and Stewart, 1972), Barry Lopez's *Apologia* (University of Georgia Press, 1998) and *Of Wolves and Men* (Touchstone, 1978) and David Jones's *Whales* (Whitecap, 1998).

Author's Note

The long-established convention of categorising published prose as fiction or non-fiction has never sat
comfortably on my shoulders, not least because as
one who produces mostly non-fiction nature writing,
I am unhappy having my work classified by what it is
not rather than what it is. (Even worse is the genre
known as 'literary non-fiction'. I cite George Mackay
Brown's observation that there is no such thing as a
good poem or a bad poem, only a poem or a mess of
words on the page. Likewise, if the writing isn't literary,
it isn't writing, is it?) Besides, as a sometimes novelist
and poet myself, and an insinuator of elements of fiction
and poetry into my so-called non-fiction books, the
instinct to take creative liberties within the framework
of known events is often irresistible.

So it is with *The Winter Whale*. In particular, I have
put words into the mouths of real nineteenth-century
people and I have read between the lines of old newspaper cuttings and ransacked clues to make assump-
tions about the character of some of them. There are

two reasons for this. One is that (I hope!) it helps to pin down and personalise something of the attitude to the natural world in general and whales in particular that prevailed in Victorian Scotland. The other is simply that any writer likes to write, to ask himself 'how will it be if I try this?' So the liberties taken are all my own.

Jim Crumley
May 2008

Chapter 1

How Whales Die

The defect that hinders communication betwixt them
and us, why may it not be on our part as well as
theirs? 'Tis yet to determine where the fault lies that
we understand not one another, for we understand
them no more than they do us; by the same reason
they may think us beasts as we think them.

Michael de Montaigne
Essays, 1693

One hundred and twenty years ago, somewhere in the
world's oceans, an unknown harpoon gunner on a
small boat from an unknown whaling ship fired one
of the new explosive harpoons into the neck of a
bowhead whale. The weapon was basically a bomb
on a stick. It was designed to penetrate the whale's
skin and blubber, then explode deep inside the whale
a few seconds later. The theory was that it would
die at once, or at least quickly. The whale died all
right. It died off the Alaskan coast in May 2007, but
only because it had been harpooned again. It was
about 130 years old, or, to put it another way, in

late middle age. The world's media gasped at the discovery.

We know all this because the twenty-first-century whalers found the nineteenth-century harpoonist's missile still embedded in the whale, in a bone between neck and shoulder. It had lodged in what they called 'a non-lethal place', and there it remained, and over the decades the initial pain might have dulled to a vague ache or an itch the whale couldn't scratch. Perhaps it swam a million miles with that itch.

The discovery was both fascinating and troubling. The fascination is that the age of whales suddenly catapulted from scientific guesswork to public knowledge, and – as is so often the case when whales command our attention – our response has been to gasp in a kind of primitive wonder. The troubled nature of the fascination is that we have only acquired the new knowledge because our fingerprints were on the whale, or rather in it, lodged 'in a non-lethal place' between neck and shoulder. All science could date with any accuracy was the missile itself, the head of the bomb lance. Staff at an American whaling museum pinned down its manufacture to New Bedford, Massachusetts. They also know it had been in the hands of an Alaskan, because of the nature of the notches carved into the head, a system by which Alaskan whalers of the time pronounced 'ownership of the whale'.

Science got excited, because, as the man from the

whaling museum in New Bedford put it, 'no other finding has been this precise'. I suppose precision is relative when you are dealing with things that live so much longer than we do. Yet evidence 'this precise' has been around for centuries, and ignored by science because it distrusts the source.

For example, I have come across something similar in studies of wolves, and found it tellingly articulated by the American nature writer Barry Lopez in his 1978 book *Of Wolves and Men*. He was explaining why many biologists irritated him:

> The Nunamiut Eskimos, the Naskapi Indians of Labrador, the tribes of the northern plains and the North Pacific coast . . . are all, in a sense, timeless. Even those tribes we can converse with today because they happen to live in our own age are timeless; the ideas that surface in conversation with them (even inside a helicopter at two thousand feet) are ancient ideas. For the vision that guides them is not the vision that guides Western man a thousand years removed from the Age of Charlemagne. And the life they lead, you notice, tagging along behind them as they hunt, really is replete with examples of the way wolves might do things. Over thousands of years Eskimos and wolves have tended to develop the same kind of efficiency in the Arctic.
>
> It is one of the oddities of our age that much of what Eskimos know about wolves – and speak about clearly in

English, in twentieth-century terms – wildlife biologists are intent on discovering. It was this fact that made me uneasy. Later, I was made even more uneasy by how much fuller the wolf was as a creature in the mind of the modern Eskimo . . .

Meanwhile, wildlife biologists theorise about the age of a whale, explain the difficulties of assessing it scientifically, knowing in the case of this particular whale only the age of a missile lodged inside it, while Inupiat Eskimos, one of Lopez's 'tribes of the northern Pacific coast', have known – 'and spoken about clearly in English in twentieth-century terms' – that whales have twice the lifespan of a man, so that 150 years old is common, and the oldest might live to be 200 years old.

Whales and wolves are still big species in the minds of all the tribes that inhabit the northern edge of our hemisphere. Their accumulated knowledge is handed down and refined over millennia. Lopez's word 'time-less' is quite literally appropriate. They have carried it into the twenty-first century, even with helicopters and snowmobiles at their disposal, and they go on learning and refining, because – then as now – some kind of understanding of these species in particular is central to their own way of life, and because they exist within nature as one of its creatures rather than apart from it like most of the rest of us. Their knowledge was garnered and stored and passed on without computers, without radio collars, without microchips, without scientific databases. They are their own database.

People not unlike them, at least in their sensibilities, would have inhabited Britain once, for our first settlers were also coast dwellers on the rim of a continent who lived with and learned from the possibilities offered by proximity to wolf and whale, and for 5,000 years they too amassed unique knowledge. But by the time our more recent forebears built their own whaling industry, and made their wolf extinct (remarkably, at more or less the same time), the bridge to the old knowledge was broken. And after that, something ancient and unnameable only ever stirred in us when an extraordinary circumstance occurred. For example:

'Twas in the month of December, and in the year 1883,
That a monster whale came to Dundee,
Resolved for a few days to sport and play,
And devour the small fishes in the silvery Tay.

William Topaz McGonagall, self-styled Poet and Tragedian, an eccentric, perambulating Victorian historical monument of Dundee streets, is still cherished by twenty-first-century Dundee, albeit with a smirk on its face. His 'poems' abandoned all known poetic conventions and structures in pursuit of a rhyme. They are routinely derided by pompous literary critics who miss the point: they were not poems so much as his scripts for one-man performances in the howffs and halls. His raw material was the events and the personalities of the day and set-piece episodes of history. And one of his greatest hits was 'The Famous Tay Whale'. The fact that the poem exists is all that most people in twenty-first-century Dundee know about the whale that turned up and lingered in the Tay estuary in the winter of 1883–84, that and the fact that its skeleton has been suspended from the ceiling of the city's main museum more or less ever since.

Even as a child growing up in Dundee, when that skeleton first haunted my young dreams, it struck me as an odd way to display a dead whale, as if it were some preposterous species of flying fish you could only admire from below. And of course I knew nothing of the nature of its death, only that it had swum up the Tay estuary to Dundee and that it had died. Well of course it died, my childhood self reasoned, anything that old would be dead, a bit like my grandfather.

But here's a thing: if the Famous Tay Whale had been left to its own devices rather than hunted to its slow and dishonourable death in early January 1884, then paraded in death around Britain for the entertainment of vast crowds of gawping Victorians – paraded without its flesh, without its organs, without its backbone, its skin stuffed and draped over a wooden frame and stitched up again to look like a caricature of its living self – it might still be alive today.

At which thought, the twenty-first-century Inupiat shrugs in a timeless way and says:

'Of course.'

Chapter 2

The Whaling Times

Because whales are the biggest mammals, whaling is,
I feel, the biggest crime.

Roger Payne
Among Whales, 1995

Whaling is ancient. Those 'timeless' Eskimos of the
Arctic rim that Barry Lopez wrote about are thought
to have hunted whales for anything between 4,000 and
8,000 years. The Japanese are probably not far behind.
But coast dwellers everywhere in the world have known
from the beginnings of all their times that whales
occasionally beach themselves, and when they do, they
are helpless and harmless and sometimes die. They saw
the sudden, unpredictable arrivals of such 'fish' on
their doorsteps as gifts from their oceanic Gods. If they
had the tools to cut through the layer of blubber, there
was a vast store of meat at their disposal, and if they
could salt it or smoke it, there was enough to see them
through the leanest of winters. There were also bones
and baleen to fashion into other tools, weapons; sinews

for bowstrings; blubber for candles; teeth to carve into brooches, ornaments, art.

They learned how to kill the whales that did not die of their own accord, then to drive whales ashore with their boats and to kill them in the shallows. Ever since, and over several millennia, the human mind has devoted an inordinate amount of energy to the task of refining its technique for killing whales. (The Russians achieved the apocalyptic zenith of that enterprise at the end of the 1950s with the launch of two factory ships of 32,000 and 33,000 tons, the biggest whaling factory ships ever built. After 25 years of sustaining the level of slaughter necessary to offset the cost of keeping these ships afloat, they were retired, only to re-emerge a few years later as floating slaughterhouses for 10 million sheep a year on regular voyages between Australia and Russia.) Over the same period, whales have not changed their behaviour towards us. They have simply gone on being whales, being our occasional neighbours, baffling us with their many mysteries as we doubtless baffle them with ours. They have troubled us too with their benevolence towards us despite our ever more ingenious hostility, and with their colossal strength and beauty.

It is more or less agreed among whale biologists that the first commercial whalers in Europe (as opposed to the unknown, undocumented legions of thousands of years of subsistence whalers) were the Basques on the shores of the Bay of Biscay. Having more or less cleared the whales from their coastal waters, they turned to the North Atlantic on whaling expeditions 500 years ago, a pattern which was echoed in other parts of the world. They began regular operations off Iceland and Greenland. The discovery by late twentieth-century archaeologists of sixteenth-century Basque ships west of Greenland was our first glimpse of the spoor of the earliest pelagic whalers at work.

By 1600 the Basques were venturing into the Davis Strait between Greenland and Baffin Island, and north of Norway around Spitzbergen. Britain, meanwhile, was more interested in discovering the Northwest Passage, but sea captains temporarily defeated by pack ice returned home with stories of immense numbers of whales, enough to quicken the interest of maritime entrepreneurs in London who despatched the *Margaret* to Greenland in 1611, specifically to look for whales. It seems to have been a less-than-wholehearted endeavour, and after a dozen years it fizzled out. But at the same time the Dutch were amassing a formidable whaling reputation. They built a whaling town on Spitzbergen so that they could turn blubber into oil more or less where they caught whales. The statistics are breathtaking: 14,000 men, 250 vessels, and in one four-year period they killed 10,000 whales.

The inevitable consequence has had to be learned and re-learned ad infinitum and ad nauseam throughout the history of whaling – the whalers ran out of whales.

Every commercial whaling endeavour that ever failed anywhere in the world did so because of greed, greed that spawned overfishing. The whaling industry's universal commercial philosophy ensured its right to call itself the most inefficient industry of all time. It was true in the seventeenth century, it is still true in the twenty-first century among the handful of nations still enslaved to that ancient whaling addiction. Sustainable whaling interested no one. It never has.

'It is their refusal to show restraint when the evidence for the need to do so is so overwhelming that gives modern whalers their most indelibly black mark,' wrote Roger Payne. 'It is what makes them the undisputed champions of shortsightedness in the history of our species.'

Scotland dipped a tentative toe in whaling waters in 1750, belatedly for such an enterprisingly seafaring nation. A single vessel, the *Tryal*, was bought second-hand by the newly constituted Edinburgh Whaling Company and based at Leith. Its haul for its first season was no whales and four walruses, but a system of government bounties kept the enterprise afloat. Glasgow and Campbeltown followed suit the following year, although neither ever figured prominently in any rollcall of whaling ports. Dundee got involved in 1752 with the formation of the Dundee Whale Fishing Company; its first vessel, the *Dundee*, sailed the following spring. The city was already a long-established port, but its absence of whaling experience is reflected in the fact that the ship's company included six foreign harpoonists. The *Dundee* caught twenty whales in its first four seasons, all of which was sufficiently encouraging to commission a second ship, the *Grandtully*. By 1756, then, Dundee had a whaling fleet, even if it comprised only two second-hand merchant ships. From this small beginning, the city would rise to a position of European pre-eminence in the whaling industry, but that particular voyage was a long, slow and risky venture both for the crews and the shareholders whose investment turned merchant ships into whaling ships and sailors in whalers. The *Grandtully* survived only six seasons, and caught only five whales, but the *Dundee* averaged almost three a season for thirty years before she was lost, a performance that was taken as a good enough omen to name a second and eventually a third whaler after her. By 1790, Scotland had twenty-three whalers and Dundee four, but by 1823, Dundee's fleet was ten-strong, and performed spectacularly. Journalist Norman Watson wrote in *The Dundee Whalers* (2003): '. . . the safe return of all ten ships to Dundee in 1823, with the bounty of 268 whales lowering their hulls in the estuary, shines out in the firmament of star catches at this time.'

You can use language like 'the firmament of star catches' when your subject is the whalers rather than the whales. Thus, Watson can also allow himself to record, quite without irony, that: 'Come the 1890s, only half of the fleet were able to meet the expenses of their voyage from their catch. When whales were scarce as this, men fell into a depression they called whale sickness . . .'

The men were depressed. The whales were dead. The men's depression was the result of the absence of whales, an absence caused specifically by the same men who had killed so many there were none left to catch. They became depressed at the absence of more whales to kill. It sounds like the plot for a novel by Joseph Heller – *Catch 22,000*, say, or *Catch 222,222*. The invention of a disease called 'whale sickness' is just one more of the countless perversions the industry has deployed to justify the unjustifiable. It's still doing it, too. As I write this, the Japanese announce plans to kill 1,000 humpbacks in the Antarctic 'for scientific purposes'. They decline to explain the nature of the science they pursue, nor how the cause of science can be better served by studying dead whales on dry land than living ones in their natural habitat.

It is fair to say that many forces conspired against the industry and challenged its resilience. Ships and crewmen were lost every year, victims of storms and the unpredictability of ice; scurvy was ever-present; the loathed and feared press gangs raided the whalers' crews to man naval vessels, for European wars were as rife as scurvy and the whaler crews viewed both as more or less equivalent evils; privateers seized ships and catches on the whaling grounds and demanded ransom from their insurers. The owners were as philosophical as they could be about losing a ship to storms and ice; they armed their ships in response to the depredations of privateers (and the whaling crews themselves were no pushovers); and crews became adept at jumping ship just before they made port and making their own surreptitious way home across country to thwart the press gangs. None of it impeded the head of steam that fuelled the industry. The rewards were such that every risk was worth it. From the first Basques to the twenty-first century, that didn't change. A biography of Aristotle Onassis published in 1986 quoted the diary of a whaling factory ship hand: 'Killed almost only blue whales today. Woe if this leaks out.'

The biographer, Peter Evans, added:

The slaughter meant nothing to Ari except in terms of profits and adventure. He never questioned the ethics of the expedition; the whales were there for the taking. It was merely a matter of beating the opposition and grabbing as many as possible. His first expedition in 1950 had netted 'a very nice' $4.2 million. 'Whaling is the biggest dice game in the world,' he said.

I dare say he might have thought his $4.2 million shone out in the firmament of star catches.

The mid nineteenth century proved a turning point in the story of whaling, in Scotland and the wider world. The development of steam ships that brought the whaling grounds closer was quickly followed by a series of crucial inventions. First there was a new bow-mounted canon for the new steam 'catcher' boats. Then there was a sharp-ended tube that could be rammed into a dead whale to allow compressed air to be pumped into the carcase so that it didn't sink. And then the exploding harpoon arrived. In theory at least, this charming device not only attached a line between whale and boat but also killed the whale quickly by blasting its innards with shrapnel. As we have already seen, it was less than 100 per cent reliable.

The impact of all this technology on whale populations was immediate and devastating. No whaling port embraced it more enthusiastically than Dundee, where Stephen's shipbuilding yard began to build a new generation of whaling ships that were quickly in demand on both sides of the Atlantic. The *Narwhal* was the first of the new breed. She was a fully rigged, wooden-hulled, auxiliary steamer, she was built in just four months, she was instantly the envy of the whaling industry across the world and she became the template for the new Dundee fleet. Huge cheering crowds greeted every launch of every new vessel. Even now, the historical records of the time resonate with the city's pride in its whaling pre-eminence. Dundee built the ships, the engines, bred generation after generation of skippers and whalers and its reputation travelled the world. But the toll it took on whales, walruses, seals and even polar bears was frankly obscene.

The Dundee fleet quickly overtook Peterhead and Fraserburgh, which had both been early strongholds of the Scottish whaling industry, and even made an audacious cross-border raid to buy the finest ship in the Hull fleet. As Peterhead and Fraserburgh wilted under the pressure of poor catches (and doubtless its men succumbed to protracted bouts of the whale sickness), Dundee's surging industrial economy bank-rolled its fleet and the whales of the North Atlantic paid the price.

It was, of course, completely unsustainable, and – not a moment too soon – a sudden reality check overtook the industry in 1886. That year, Dundee's 15 ships brought back only 18 whales. To add to the misery, four ships were lost, and it suddenly occurred to the local newspaper, the *Advertiser*, to demand: 'Why has prosperity deserted the prosecution of the Davis Strait fishing industry?' It was the wrong question. The right question would have been 'Why have the whales deserted the Davis Strait?' And the answer was plain to see in the faces of every whaler who suffered from the whale sickness. The newspaper spoke the unspeakable: 'all appearances point to the fishing having been overdone'. Watson quotes an unnamed skipper ten years later: 'No distinction was, or could be made, in the sex or age of whales taken. Male and female, mother and sucker, were alike harpooned and cut up.'

Two years later, in 1898, Frank T. Bullen's *The Cruise of the Cachalot Round the World after Sperm Whales* rubbished the idea that no such distinction was possible, in the most graphic manner imaginable:

The harpooner rose, darted once, twice, then gave a yell of triumph that ran re-echoing all around in a thousand eerie vibrations . . . But for all the notice taken by the whale, she might never have been touched. Close nestled to her side was a youngling of not more, certainly, than five days old, which sent up its baby-spout every now and then about two feet into the air. One long, wing-like fin embraced its small body, holding it close to the massive breast of the tender mother, whose only care seemed to be to protect her young, utterly regardless of her own pain and danger. If sentiment were ever permitted to interfere with such operations as ours, it might well have done so now; for while the calf continually sought to escape from the enfolding fin, making all sorts of puny struggles in the attempt, the mother scarcely moved from her position, although streaming with blood from a score of wounds. Once, indeed, as a deep-searching thrust entered her very vitals, she raised her massy flukes

17

high in the air with an apparently involuntary movement of agony; but even in that dire time she remembered the possible danger to her young one, and laid the tremendous weapon as softly down upon the water as if it were a fan.

So, in the most perfect quiet, with scarcely a writhe, nor any sign of flurry, she died, holding the calf to her side until her last vital spark had fled, and left it to a swift despatch with a single lance-thrust. No slaughter of a lamb ever looked more like murder. Nor, when the vast bulk and strength of the animal was considered, could a mightier example have been given of the force and quality of maternal love . . .

But sentiment never was permitted 'to interfere with operations such as ours'. That meticulously executed 'murder' was simply symptomatic of the nature of the industry, an industry which, by the last few weeks of 1883, had created in Dundee the climate of reputation and public opinion in which one more particular murder was about to be executed.

Every spring, the city's whaling fleet sailed north to the whaling grounds, and every spring and summer they plundered the whales in their breeding grounds. But what died, what sullied even a reputation won on the back of killing so many thousands of whales, was a lost juvenile whale that fate sent into the city's home waters, a winter whale. But then, as the skipper said, no distinction was, or could be made, in the sex or age of whales taken. Male and female, mother and sucker were alike harpooned and cut up. Likewise the spring whale, the summer whale, the winter whale.

Chapter 3

A Whale Arrives

So the monster whale did sport and play
Among the innocent little fishes in the beautiful Tay,
Until he was seen by some men one day
And they resolved to catch him without delay.

William McGonagall
'The Famous Tay Whale', 1884

The fields of Angus and Fife that late autumn and early winter of 1883 smelled insufferably of dead fish. The North Sea seethed with shoals of young herring. East-coast fishing boats hauled them out by the ton. When their markets had bought all they could buy and the people had eaten all they could eat, and still the herrings came and came, thick as waves on a flowing tide, they sold them to the local farmers, who spread them on their fields as manure. The sheer volume of fish doubt-less explained why so many wandered into the wide estuaries of the Tay and the Forth rather than pursuing a southward migration down the North Sea. And in their wake they lured a flotilla of predators, notably small whales and porpoises, and these in turn brought shoals of people to the outlying shores of the firths to watch the spectacle. It went on for weeks. But then, some time in the second half of November, there among the predators was one of the great whales, a humpback, and from the moment fate aligned it with the Firth of Tay it was destined for a short life, a long and brutal death, and 125 years of undying fame.

The herring shoals were why it lingered, and the shallower waters of the estuary would make them easier to catch than the depths of the open sea, and that would explain why it travelled as far upstream as Dundee, but why it was in the North Sea at all is a mystery, one of those inexplicable occurrences that constantly punctuate – and help to underpin – our fascination with whales. Humpbacks prefer the oceanic breadths of the Atlantic and the Pacific for their more or less endless migrations up and down and across the globe to and from their breeding grounds, and by the autumn of 1883, no humpback had been seen in the Tay estuary for more than 60 years.

Roger Payne, a whale biologist with an admirable and untypical sense of wonder towards his life's work, wrote in his enlightened and enlightening book, *Among Whales*:

One reason whales maintain such a hold on our imaginations seems to be their omnipossibility – their unexpected and unpredictable appearances off all coasts, invariably arriving on their own schedules, showing up for reasons we do not understand.

Though we distinguish between the Pacific Ocean, the Atlantic Ocean, the Indian Ocean, etc., there is really only one ocean, and it holds all the whales that exist . . . Whales can pass along your coast, or come into any harbour or bay that is deep enough to float them, no matter where you live . . . and sometimes they do. When it happens, it always sends a message that speaks directly – one capable of setting up waves that propagate right into the core of your very being.

Ah, but that's now, now that we have invented Greenpeace and embraced the concept of conservation, and learned to admire whales and let them into our hearts. In November 1883, the humpback whale that bore hard to starboard into the Tay estuary set up waves that propagated right into the core of the whaling industry. Whaling had begun to decline throughout Britain, and the days when every part of the whale found a market were gone: oil from blubber had been used for margarine and soap and lighting, more oil was extracted from flesh and bones, liver oil had medicinal uses, and what was left was processed for cattle feed. The baleen plates, the long strainers in the jaws of the so-called baleen whales (as opposed to toothed whales), were what you might call the mainstay of the corset industry. Whalebone was used to make piano keys, among many other

things. World traveller and nature writer Peter Mat-
thiessen voiced the distaste of millions: 'Nothing is
wasted but the whale itself.'

But in Dundee in 1883 whaling was still booming,
because the city had its own colossal market. Dundee
was the global epicentre of the jute industry then, and
that industry needed a particular lubricant that softened
the jute fibres and made them supple before they were
spun – whale oil, and it was worth more than £50 a ton
to the whalers. So the city had its own whaling fleet, the
biggest in Britain by then, the ship owners were Dundee
merchants, the captains and the crews were almost all
Dundee seamen. Their reputation travelled the whaling
world – they were the best in the business. What sealed
the fate of the Famous Tay Whale was that when it
arrived off Dundee, the city's whaling fleet was laid up
for the winter. Dundee was host to 700 whalers with
nothing to do. An anonymous 1884 pamphlet, titled
'The History of the Whale', put it thus: 'The Tay was
scarcely the place for whales to select as a playground.'

That perception, that the humpback was 'playing'
under the noses of its sworn enemy, set it apart from
other whales in Dundee's story, and gave an edge to all
that followed. It was an instant celebrity with the
crowds that gathered on beaches and other shoreline
vantage points, and a slowly smouldering source of
resentment and then frustration to the idle seamen. The
city was familiar enough with whales, or at least with

dead and butchered ones being unloaded on the dockside, and many a Dundee family watched the breadwinner disappear over the horizon every spring, bound for the Arctic whaling grounds. And like every whaling community the world over, those same families weighed the grim balance sheet that set financial profit against human loss of life. The blackest hour had come in 1836: that whaling season over 70 men were lost from two ships and 100 Dundee children lost their fathers. But the loss of whale life troubled no-one.

Then suddenly, here was what it was all about, a monster of the northern deep (and the word 'monster' is everywhere in contemporary written accounts) coughed up on their own doorstep by that same sea that routinely claimed the lives of their loved ones. Among the cheers and the jeers, and the relentless taunts to those hauled-out seamen they knew and loved, there were also silent, head-shaking moments of bewilderment and wonder. Why here, of all places? And oh, the raw and fearless beauty of the beast! But then the whalers knew such moments themselves, even in the killing fields of the northern ocean, even as they closed on a whale and readied the harpoons, they could find themselves moved by the sheer presence of their quarry, by those 'waves that propagated right into the heart of their very being'. Not that it ever stopped them launching the harpoon.

And the humpback is perhaps the most spectacular of all whales. Its habit of breaching (leaping almost

24

vertically from the water, turning onto its back or side in the air, waving its long pectoral fins like handless arms as though in greeting, then the colossal splash-down), allied to the almost unbearable grace of the hugely flourished tail as it submerges, has made the humpback the modern whale-watcher's favourite whale. And lest you don't have the dimensions of a humpback whale at your fingertips, this is – precisely (there would be a great deal of measuring of this particular whale in the weeks ahead) – what turned up in the Tay: length, 40 feet (so not fully grown); maximum girth, 24 feet; minimum girth next to the tail, 4 feet 9 inches; distance from point of snout to eye, 8 feet 10 inches; from eye to eye across the top of the head, 7 feet 9 inches; eyeball diameter, 4 inches; distance from centre of eye to ear, 1 foot 8 inches; distance from snout to blowholes, 6 feet 7 inches (there were two blowholes, each 12 inches long, 'arranged in the form of a spearhead'); jaw at widest point, 10 feet 2 inches; length of lower jaw, 11 feet 6 inches; length of pectoral fin, 12 feet; greatest breadth of pectoral fin, 2 feet 8 inches; distance from snout to dorsal fin, 25 feet 7 inches; dorsal fin, 18 inches long, 8 inches high; width of tail, 17 feet 4 inches; weight, 26 tons 8 cwts. And let's not corrupt any of that by metricating its splendidly imperial bulk.

At first, the mood was one of carnival, albeit one happed in coats and scarves and bunnets and gloves.

Each day the whale turned up, put on a show of breaching, blowing (and at each breaching and blowing the crowds roared and ooh-ed and aah-ed their delight), and then the lingering gesture of the huge poised tail before the whale submerged would silence them, and they would feel something else they could not name.

Then the long pause – where did it go?

How can something that size disappear?

Then it would burst up through the surface of the river again like a clown bursting through a paper hoop, but a clown the size of a house and a hoop more than a mile wide, and the cheers could be heard from Broughty Ferry on the Dundee side of the river to Tayport on the Fife side, where there was another smaller crowd, and more cheers. If you had heard but not seen from an inland part of the city, you might have thought you were listening to the crowd at a great football match.

And it was sport for them all, it was different, spectacular, astonishing and free. And then the tide would turn and the whale would turn with it and retreat to its mysterious deep-sea sanctuary, and that only intensified its allure in the minds of the crowds that waved it out beyond Broughty Ferry's wave-butting castle, then thrust their hands deep into their coat pockets and turned for home, and the talk at the kitchen tables and coal fires of Dundee was full of the whale.

Where had it come from?

How big was it?

How much did it weigh?

And how long would it live with the whaler lads in town, muttering darkly into their whisky glasses?

Their best guesses in answer to that particular question were measured in hours and days, certainly not weeks and months, but while they knew, most of them, about how whales were killed and what happened to them after that (for it had been a part of their city's story for 130 years by then), they knew little enough about how a whale lived, what resources it could call on. And two weeks later it was still there, still turning up for its feed, still putting on a show, and the crowds goaded the whalers to take a hand in the whale's game, to do something about it if they dared. And then it disappeared as if it had never been, and after a week of dwindling, hopeful crowds, then no crowds at all, it was suddenly the stuff of memory and they set about polishing its legend, and the whaler lads were left to kick their heels, and to console each other that maybe they should have launched a boat or two and they might have written their own legend. But for ten days, the Firth of Tay was a blank page. And then it came back.

The crowds redoubled. Everyone had a theory about where it had gone. Some said Arbroath, some said Holland, some said it had gone to cheer up the keepers at the Bell Rock lighthouse that stands 20 miles out to sea from Dundee on its rock plinth and appears on the clearest days as a horizon smudge, and on the clearest nights as the lowest star in the sky, a star that blinks to a known rhythmic pattern. Did the whale know it for what it was, or just as the lowest star in the sky?

'As a consequence of their great size, whales escape much turmoil,' wrote Roger Payne. 'With increasing size comes increasing serenity. With size comes tranquillity. For a whale, a passing thunderstorm is but the footfall of an ant, and a full gale an annoying jiggling of his pleasant bed. If you were a whale, all but the grandest of things would pass beneath your notice.'

The Famous Tay Whale could not know, of course, that it was playing with that grandest of things, fire.

Chapter 4

The Hunt

Then the people together in crowds did run,
Resolved to capture the whale and to have some fun!
So small boats were launched on the silvery Tay,
While the monster of the deep did sport and play.

Oh it was a most fearful and beautiful sight,
To see it lashing the water with its tail all its might,
And making the water ascend like a shower of hail,
With one lash of its ugly and mighty tail.

Then the water did descend on the men in the boats,
Which wet their trousers and also their coats;
But it only made them more determined to catch the whale,
But the whale shook at them its tail.

William McGonagall
'The Famous Tay Whale'

The whale gave another practical proof of his saga-
city today by keeping well out of reach of his
pursuers. He was seen in the early morning disporting in the river off Newport for a short time, and no
sooner was his presence made known in Dundee
than a whaleboat was launched and started off in
pursuit. Another whaleboat manned by volunteers
eager for sport, with fire-arms, and determined to try

the effects of powder and ball upon his carcase, followed suit. It is said that a steam-launch also joined in the chase, when the 'finner', evidently thinking discretion was the better part of valour, set his nose eastward, and made for the mouth of the river. Since then up till the afternoon, I can find no one who has seen him. But it naturally occurs to ordinary people to ask the question, Is this whale to be allowed to come up the river day after day in front of the good town of Dundee, and, before the crews and captains of a dozen whalers, flaunt its tail and, figuratively speaking, put its flipper to its nose at them without a determined effort on their part to throw salt on its tail and lay it up on the beach, so that the general public may have a look at him?

I don't believe it is true, as some people say, that our whaling captains don't care to tackle a 'finner'. Wild stories are being told of their dragging whaleboats made fast to them for perhaps fifty miles from the place where they were harpooned, and they are even declared to round on their tormentors and knock a boat to pieces by a flip of their tail. There is no doubt at any rate that the chief difficulty the whalers have to contend with is to get within striking distance of the whale in the river. No harpooner will risk a shot at a greater distance than twenty-five yards and they prefer to be within half that range before they shoot. It will be by an exceptional stroke of luck if our marine winter visitor allows them to come to such close quarters as that, and there can be little doubt that a bad quarter of an hour will follow for those who make themselves fast to such a sturdy, lively and erratic animal.

Dundee Advertiser, December 1883
'The Eye-Witness to the Chase'

The Hunt

Except for our killing of each other, what other
mammal have we killed with greater savagery?

Roger Payne
Among Whales

If only the whale had stayed away when it disappeared
after those first two weeks, retraced its journey back up
the North Sea and into the Pentland Firth where it
would have felt the contrary currents of the Atlantic
between Caithness and Orkney and the great oceanic
liberation beyond, resumed the ancient routine of its
tribal migrations to and from the breeding grounds,
5,000 miles there, 5,000 miles back . . . if only:

It might have lived another 150 years, perhaps
longer.

It might have swum another million miles, perhaps
further.

It might have increased its overall length by another
10–15 feet to something over 50 feet.

It might have increased its weight by another 8 or 9
tons to around 35 tons.

It might have sired a new dynasty of humpback
whales.

McGonagall would have been short of a poem,
Dundee's museum would have been short of its star
exhibit, and even in Dundee most of us could have lived
with that. My old home town would also have spared
me my uneasy inheritance, and I could certainly have

lived without that. But the whale returned for reasons best known to itself, and what followed was an inglorious moment in the city's story, one quite unmitigated by the passage of time.

It seems from this distance that the whalers were reluctant to launch a hunt. The whale swam unmolested in their home waters for two weeks. Perhaps it was simply that they were enjoying not being at sea, a few weeks of well-earned rest from the colossal labours of their trade. It may have been that they were not in their working habitat of the North Atlantic. Perhaps the ship owners saw little merit in rounding up crews in holiday mood to pursue a single whale in front of a crowd of thousands, a circumstance that turned their notoriously dangerous deep-sea trade into a game in the comparative shallows of the firth. And it may be that they judged the humpback not worth the effort commercially, for its layer of fat is thin and yields little of the precious oil, and it was known among whalers that the carcase of a dead humpback usually sinks. (By comparison, the Greenland right whale's fat layer is thick and therefore valuable, and it floats in death – hence 'right' whale, the right one to catch.) That fact alone – the humpback's poor commercial value to the Dundee whalers – condemned the hunt. There was almost nothing to be gained by it. Even by the ethical standards of the time, there was no reason for that whale to die, no reason to launch the boats other than an opportunity to put on a show. By the time the whalers overcame their reluctance to do just that and finally launched their boats, the whale had become the doomed objective of a blood sport with a watching crowd in an arena the size of the firth. It was as blatant as a bullfight.

Alas, the whalers were off form, their skills blunted by the lay-off perhaps, or hampered by the makeshift and half-hearted nature of the endeavour. Day after day then, their boats put out from Dundee, and some days they got close to the whale and some days they did not, and some days they could not find it at all. And even when they did get close their aim was indifferent, and the suspicion arose and gained currency amid the taunts of the shoreline masses that the whale was having a laugh. The whalers' discomfort was not helped by dozens of amateurs who took to their own boats and fired all manner of missiles in the general direction of the whale from improbable distances. That anonymous pamphleteer assessed the mood in those last few days of 1883 thus:

Day after day the whale boats rowed over the firth and fired guns and harpoons and blessings and other things at the fish, which, when the tide turned, blandly turned with it, and left the wearied hunters to enjoy their well-earned rest and the blisters which the healthy exercise raised on their hands. Six weeks of this sort of thing disgusted the crews, but appeared to have an elevating effect on the whale, for it frequently treated the spectators on the shore to an exhibition of antics which, while amusing the onlookers, did not accord well with the calm dignity which ought to distinguish an animal weighing twenty-six tons. The immunity from danger which the fish had enjoyed had the effect of blunting its wariness, and its familiarity with the previous bad marksmanship of the Dundee whalers led to its ruin.

The whale ran out of luck on Hogmanay.

The day dawned grey and still. Thick cloud had hauled down in the night across the summits of the low hills of Angus and Fife on either side of the Tay estuary. The promise of worse weather to come hung bleakly on the air. In those conditions, the blowing hiss of a humpback whale and the thin cloud of fine white spray it sends up to 20 feet in the air would have advertised its presence for miles around. Some of the Dundee whalers, now eager for the denouement, were on the river early, searching for the whale. The conditions while they lasted were as good as they could reasonably expect in the short daylight of their northern midwinter. A whaleboat from the whaler *Chieftain* was out first, though its effectiveness might have been compromised by at least one member of the listed crew: 'Captain Gellatly; Tennant, his mate; Seamen James Watson, James Allan, Thomas Hutton; and a commercial traveller, Pat Reid from Broughty Ferry'. The whaleboats were open, 28 feet long, and had a crew of six – four rowers, a helmsman and a harpoonist. The *Chieftain*'s boat was soon joined by a whaleboat from the *Thetis* and a steam launch from the *Polar Star*.

Captain Gellatly anchored to the Newcombe buoy. His crew watched the placid water. Then the whale breached and then she blew. And then – another characteristic of humpbacks – it settled down and lay dead still on the surface. And in the minds of the whalers, it said: 'Come and get me.' The *Thetis* whaleboat and the steam launch edged stealthily downstream, closing in on the whale at little more than the speed of the river.

In the bow of the launch, harpoonist James Lyons felt the old familiar dryness in his throat, the old familiar sweating dampness on his palms. But there was a bad and unfamiliar taste in his mouth. He was uneasy about this. The small dorsal fin and a broad black curve of whale back broke the surface slowly, like breathing, and suddenly the situation was grotesque, and somehow absurd with the low Fife shore of the Tay for a backdrop. The sense of an unearthly dream flickered in his mind, the voice of the helmsman and the muted rumble of the engine no more than accessories of the dream. He moved his hands automatically into position on the harpoon gun and the coldness of it snapped him out of the dream, but did not change his mood.

Fifty yards.

He'd fired from further than that on a berserk deck in

the Arctic Ocean in a grey and green landscape of iceberg and waves taller than his boat was long, and found his mark, confident of his skill, reading the sea, perfecting his timing over 20 seasons. But this . . . the whale lying as leisurely as the Tay lightship at anchor in slack water, unperturbed by the boats' creeping advance, and the eeriness of having all the landmarks of home at every compass point . . .

She can't even dive.

She has eight fathoms of water beneath her if that, and she must be seven fathoms long herself . . . [the whales were all 'she' to the crews, a mark of respect otherwise reserved for the ships themselves] . . . *she has barely enough water to float her.*

One clean hit, lady, and it's over. Then die quickly. Know that I don't like this.

Know that I would rather you sped for the sea now and we meet again in the summer some day in Greenland's waters, and we match each other fairly, strength for strength, you in your element and I in mine.

[The helmsman's voice again, distant and indistinct] *What's he saying? Who cares? I'm sorry for this, lady. But it's out of my hands.*

God, let her die quickly.

Thirty yards.

The whale arches its back, a gentle flex, and the fin rises a foot more out of the water, which signals a shallow dive. He fires as far ahead of the arch as he

dares and knows he has hit its shoulder and hurt it, and
he waits for it to react, and he shouts:

She feels it!

He shouts without looking back over his shoulder,
watching the whale, waiting for it to react, willing it to
convulse and die. Instead, it begins without fuss to tow
the launch forward. He sees the small bow wave ripple
out beneath him and groans and mutters a black oath
into his beard. He turns to speak to the helmsman and
sees that instead of hoisting the flag that would signal a
hit, he had hoisted a coalsack.

The bastard didn't even bring a flag!

He spits.

He hears the crowds cheer on the shore. He looks
over his other shoulder to Dundee a mile away.

*They saw the sack! They laughed at it! Why wouldn't
they laugh at it?*

*Aye, but they cheer and throw their caps in the air
now that they know she's hit, now they know she feels
it, and they clap and hug each other and dance up and
down.*

He spits again. He sees the boats pouring out from
the shore, all of them crammed with spectators eager for
a closer view. He mutters a line of Burns:

Out the hellish legion sallied . . .

*She's rising to blow. This time the spray from her will
be red. They'll see that, the bloodthirsty bastards. She
feels it. The line's holding. At least I've done my job. Do*

*your worst lady. It's in your hands now. And God's.
God let her die quickly.*

God did not let the whale die quickly. The launch had
run out only seven or eight fathoms of line so she
steamed squarely in the reddening wake of the whale.
Now that the whale was easy meat, the *Chieftain*
whaleboat re-entered the fray, manoeuvring between
the launch and the whale to fire point-blank a second
harpoon. Meanwhile the *Thetis* whaleboat had attached a line to the launch and now the whale towed
all three boats. And with the explosion of the second
harpoon inside her, 'the whale shook at them its tail' as
McGonagall put it. That tail, remember, was 17 feet 4
inches wide, rather wider than the whaleboat that had
just attached itself to her innards. As the whale brought
the physical resources of its 26 tons to bear on the effort
of raising then smashing down its tail into the sea, it
raised a splash that drenched the boat and its crew from
harpoonist to helmsman, drenched them not with what
McGonagall called 'a shower of hail' but with a cascade
of its own blood. In the bow of the launch, James Lyons
bit into his own tongue in his anger, and when he spat
again the blood of his own mouth mingled in the sea
with the blood of the whale. On the shore and in the
flotilla of spectators' boats, the crowds realised that one
of the whaleboats was now being towed *ahead* of the
steam launch, and that she must be fast to the whale
and they cheered again. Their cries and applause rolled

across the still, grey waters of the Tay to where the seamen laboured in a troublesome oasis of reddening turbulence.

For the whale had suddenly changed tactics. It was galvanised by the new pain and the huge deadweight of the three boats. It charged in a series of zig-zags, then in a tight U-turn that took it upstream again, but almost at once it seemed to realise the error of that ploy and turned again for the open sea, and of course the three boats followed its every move, for while the whale's strength and the harpoon lines held they were as helpless as leaves in a November gale.

And then the whaleboat harpoon drew, and it was suddenly denied the power of the whale's engine room. Its four oarsmen could make no headway at all against the strongly flowing tide. They fell further and further back from the heat of battle as the whale dragged it eastwards. Captain Gellatly had no choice but to order a return to port, the *Chieftain* reduced to the rank of the *Crestfallen*, its crewmen under no illusions about the kind of reception the crowds would afford them back in Dundee. But Pat Reid, commercial traveller of Broughty Ferry, would have a rare story to tell on his rounds among his landlubber clients about the one that got away.

Now the *Thetis* whaleboat, which was still being towed by the launch, pulled ahead to put another harpoon into the whale. The first effort failed, but a second held. Yet still the whale swam on, out through the widening jaws of the firth, heading for the open sea, constantly twisting and changing direction as it tried to shed its burden. For the whale, life had been reduced to a single overwhelming simplicity. The agonies it now endured were matched only by its brute strength, and while that strength lasted it fuelled the urge to survive, to shake off the lines that held it to the boats, to swim free of its burden, to dive deep, to let time pass, and then to heal.

Chapter 5

Escape

And they laughed and grinned just like wild baboons,
While they fired at him their sharp harpoons:
But when struck with the harpoons he dived below,
Which filled his pursuers' hearts with woe:

Because they guessed they had lost a prize,
Which caused the tears to well up in their eyes;
And in that their anticipation was only right,
Because he sped on to Stonehaven with all his might...

William McGonagall
'The Famous Tay Whale'

A Word for the Whale
Is there no one to put in a word for the poor whale?
I don't think I can be called squeamish, yet your
account of the whale hunt in the Tay has given me
'a bit of a turn'. I look upon the treatment that whale
has received as an outrage on nature and humanity,
and I would to Heaven that the Christian Nimrods
who had all the glory of it had got three days and
three nights in the whale's belly for their pains! What
harm was the beast doing? Harm! What greater New
Year's treat to thousands of idlers, old and young,
than to see the noble creature leaping and spouting in

41

the Tay! And to have swam the ocean stream all the way from the frigid zone to be gashed and gored with lances to make sport for the Philistines of Dundee! And then that long, desperate, agonising struggle to shake itself free from its murderers . . . The necessities of trade cannot be pleaded in extenuation; either greed or cruel instinct is to blame; and I am much mistaken if it be not widely felt to have been a wanton outrage on the innocence and majesty of nature . . .

A. Stephenson, Edinburgh
Letter to the *Scotsman* newspaper, January 1884

Captain Charles Yule commanded international respect as well as ships. Wherever men and whales coincided in the northern oceans of the world, whenever whalers met and discussed the business of wresting whales from Arctic waters, the names of a handful of Dundee sea captains punctuated the conversation as reliably and vividly as the Bell Rock light lit the night sky. Captain Yule belonged to that seagoing aristocracy. But he was an exception to the rule that they lived and died for the job, and died young at that. He had certainly gone to sea when he was very young, he captained the whalers, notably the Dundee-built *Esquimaux* (and eyed the prospect of taking her to the North Pole in 1873), but then he became harbourmaster to the Port of Dundee at the age of around 43, retired at the age of 80, and died in Dundee in 1936 at the age of 100. It is fair to say that when the humpback turned up in the Tay in the last few weeks of 1883, there was no one in

Dundee, and few anywhere in the world, who knew more about whales and how to catch them.

He was naturally intrigued. He had first seen the whale from his office window, for it would be a poor harbourmaster's office whose window was not full of the river and the business of ships, and this harbourmaster's office was not poor. And he had recognised the whale for what it was without the telescope, not by its leap or its tail or by the way it blew, but just by the way it lay dead still on the water, a low-lying black hull on the slate-gray winter river that was not a craft and not a familiar fragment of the river's landscape. He knew two things in his life with a quite consummate expertise: the landscape of the Tay estuary at every conceivable and inconceivable state of the tide and every season of the year and hour of the day or night, and what every characteristic of all the whales of the northern ocean looked like, sounded like, felt like, smelled like. And one November morning he walked over to the window the way he did perhaps fifty times a day and he saw the river, and there was a stationary whale in it where there had been none a quarter of an hour before. He looked without speaking for a few seconds then told the empty room, 'Humpback!', then he confirmed his diagnosis with the telescope already mounted by the window.

'Humpback!'

He had spoken the word softly as if there was someone standing by his shoulder who should be told, but rather the fact of speaking its name aloud was required for his mind to accept what his eyes were telling him. Yet why should he be surprised? He was sure that sooner or later that flowing tide of fish must summon one of the great whales lingering off Norway. Perhaps he had not expected a humpback, for they foraged so rarely down the North Sea, but there was no argument about what he saw in the circle of the glass – that old familiar colossal indifference, the tribal aloofness.

He spoke louder over his shoulder, his eye still at the telescope:

'Ritchie! Come and see this!'

From the next room, a scrape of a chair, a heavy ledger closing, his clerk Ritchie's slow footfall:

'Coming!'

Even as he watched, the whale stirred, it rose on the water, then the tail . . . the wonder of it, the graceful heave of it . . . then the whole creature slid under, and in the glass were ripples and bubbles, and then there was just the slate-grey river.

'What is it?'

'Nothing. Sorry. My mistake.'

His clerk turned back to his desk with a grunt and a furrowed brow. Captain Yule did not make mistakes, at least not with *that* telescope and *that* river, and then he heard Ritchie's footfall pause in the doorway and turn, then his voice:

'No, you didn't.'

'Didn't what?'

'Make a mistake. Not with that.'

Ritchie had gestured at the telescope. The captain turned and smiled.

'No. No, you're right. I just saw a ghost.'

'A ghost?'

'A whale.'

'A whale or a ghost?'

'A humpback whale in the other end of the glass. I spent 25 seasons killing whales and the humpback was the one I never liked to kill, but I killed them anyway, I killed them and then I ordered others to kill them. Finally I came home, believing I had killed my last whale. Harbourmaster of the port from which I sailed to kill whales – it's a fine distinction, wouldn't you say? And now a humpback has turned up just outside my harbour. Why else but to haunt me? It's what ghosts are for.'

'I never met a ghost, Captain, but the whale is here to eat fish.'

'But a humpback, Ritchie, *here*! It's an ill omen. This town will spill the whale's blood on the front doorstep if it gets the chance. On my watch.'

'You're taking this very personally, Captain. The whale might swim back out to sea when the tide turns.'

'Yes, it might, and I hope so, but I doubt it . . . so much food, such easy pickings. They sing, you know.'

'They sing? I thought that was just seals.'

'No, the humpbacks also sing. At home, in the Arctic Ocean, they sing. They sing *at* you and yes, it's personal.'

The two men stood beside the telescope as they talked, the hauled-out mariner and the landlubber clerk, and, as they looked out over the estuary, the whale burst the skin of the river apart, turned in the air, raised a flipper and waved it, then it crashed back into the water and vanished, and the river convulsed and shook itself then smoothed itself and layered the whale-chaos with a veneer of slate-grey calm. Ritchie, who had heard a thousand whale stories but never seen a humpback breach, turned to the captain and in his careful clerk's voice he said:

'Do you know, I think you're right. It *is* personal. That whale just waved to you.'

He tried to make it sound light-hearted. But the normally cheerful harbourmaster wore an expression as unfathomable and distant as a Newfoundland fog.

For two weeks then, Captain Charles Yule watched with growing unease as the built city that massed greyly uphill and inland behind his office emptied every day and the natives crowded down to the shore, the masses thickening daily and growing hoarse.

'Listen to them,' he told Ritchie, 'they are as unreasoning as drunks; they're a hunting pack without hounds.'

46

And then, a week after the whale vanished from the river, a week of the-one-that-got-away leg-pulling and legend-polishing, Ritchie saw him at the telescope and ventured a passing remark from the door:

'Nothing?'

'Nothing.'

'She's gone, hasn't she? She's truly gone, to Norway, to the North Atlantic, perhaps, but she has gone.'

'No, Ritchie. She has not gone.'

'You sound sure.'

'I know whales.'

'Well, you're wrong about this one. Why don't you accept it? She's gone. It's been a week.'

'No. She's out by the Bell Rock, working the shoals as they divide round the reef. She'll head them off for a few more days, then she'll turn and drive them in; she remembers where she's been, and some whales just like being in estuaries, this is one of them. If only she hadn't chosen this estuary. She'll be back. And when she does come back, I fear the hunting pack will have their hounds.'

'What, they'll launch the boats and kill her here? Surely not!'

'They'll try. But it's harder than they think. They'll run out of space, they'll run out of room to manoeuvre – the currents and the sandbanks and the other shipping, and every clown with his own boat will be out there trying to show them up and firing God knows what into the poor damned whale. If they get anywhere near her at all, that is.'

'The poor damned whale? You'd better not go into the Arctic Whaler talking like that. You'll be out of a job by New Year.'

Again, Ritchie had tried to lighten the mood in the harbourmaster's office but the mindset of Captain Charles Yule was still far-off and fogbound. It was hardly improved by subsequent events, for, as we have seen, the whale did return, the hunting pack got their hounds, the boats were launched and the confines and currents and maritime traffic of the Firth confounded their efforts. As the weeks passed and the whale eluded them all, messages of derisory greeting began to arrive from other whaling ports all over Britain. The whaling community was a tight one and news travelled fast within it. Word of the Dundee fleet's self-inflicted wound was transmitted gleefully from one end of the east coast to the other, and the harbourmaster's office was the destination of most of their jokes at Dundee's expense.

By Hogmanay, the harbourmaster's embarrassment was acute, his mood was wretched and the prospect of a holiday and seeing in the New Year with a houseful of friends and family was as distant as Cape Farewell.* Then word reached his office that the whale had been

---

* The southern tip of Greenland, a whaler's landmark in the northern ocean.

hit, then that it had been hit again, and that they had hoisted a coal sack for want of a flag. And now, he thought, it is the whalers themselves who act like clowns. A coal sack! What on earth? . . . And then he knew from the cheers that she had been hit again. And he echoed the prayer of the harpoonist: 'God, let her die quickly.' And he guessed that was a doomed prayer when he heard that the whale was towing the convoy in the general direction of Holland.

Captain Yule considered the situation. It was noon. There were perhaps four hours of usable daylight left. The weather was about to get worse and if the whale made it far enough out into the open sea as it began to roughen, then the odds would swing in favour of the whale. Not that it was likely to survive, just that the chances were the lines would part, the whale would escape to die slowly, quietly, alone and God knows where, the whalers would return home empty-handed and beaten, someone else would probably benefit from the whale's eventual death, and Dundee's reputation on the world's whaling stage would take a hammering. None of it made an attractive prospect.

Perhaps there was still time to retrieve the situation, a single decisive gesture that shifted the balance of power quickly, and determined the final outcome in favour of the whalers, the city and (he was not indifferent in the matter) the reputation of the harbourmaster. The whale must be slowed, it must be weakened so that the killing blows could be landed, the hand-driven lances deep into heart and lungs so that she bled to death quickly. Captain Yule ordered the harbour's hefty steam tug *Iron King* into the fray and he boarded her himself. If anyone knew how to stop the whale in its tracks, he did. He would. The crowds at the docks spotted the new activity, guessed its meaning and cheered the *Iron King* out into the Tay, the cavalry riding decisively into the heat of battle. The deed was as good as done.

The *Iron King* reached the strange, whale-powered convoy at around 3 p.m. Captain Yule decided to take two of the lines on board the tug and leave the third fast to one of the whaleboats. Thus, the whale was now towing the *Iron King*, the steam launch, and the two remaining whaleboats, and their various crews might have been forgiven for thinking their combined might would have stopped the whale in its tracks, if not actually stopped it dead. But with the colossal drag of the *Iron King* added to the whale's malevolent retinue, it simply swam on, its strength and resolve undiminished while the light faded, the weather worsened and the whalers' spirits sank. They had not anticipated a night at sea and they had made no provision for one, nor had they anticipated that the whale would outlast them. They had no food, no drink, no lights and no spare harpoons, lances or rockets. They watched the light fade, they watched the dark shapelessness of the whale that towed them to God knows what fate, they watched the weather bear down on them and they felt the sea grow uneasy – as if even the sea itself was about to visit its disapproval on them for all that had befallen one of its own creatures. Then, at 4.30 p.m., the two lines attached to the tug snapped. The situation, entirely of the whalers' own making, was now quite out of control. The *Iron King* took the last line on board and also the crews of the whaleboats to reduce the possibility of collisions in the dark. And in the dark the whale could see, and in the dark the whale pursued its course, and in the dark the open sea embraced the whale because it was finally home again, and in the dark the sea set about reclaiming its own.

The *Dundee Advertiser*'s voracious coverage of the Tay Whale considered that night under the headlines THE WHALE HUNT IN THE TAY and ESCAPE OF THE MONSTER:

At this time the steamer [the steam tug *Iron King*] was between the Bell Rock and the Buoy of Tay, and unfortunately there were no spare harpoons, lances or rockets on board the boats, so that nothing further could be done to secure the capture of the whale, which was therefore allowed to tow the tug and the boats at its own will. At times its strength seemed to be spent, but after a short breathing space it acquired renewed energy, and darted away, towing the tug and boats at a rapid speed. Throughout the night it continued its course, describing a

sort of circle, and dragging the steamer from the Bell
Rock to within a few miles of Scurdy Ness Lighthouse,
Montrose. During the night the weather was very thick,
and considerable anxiety was felt by those on board the
steamer, but as the line showed no signs of giving way
they were confident of the success of their labours . . .

If it seems extraordinary that such an experienced
group of seafarers mounted such an ill-prepared expedition to catch such a familiar adversary, apparently
discounting the possibility that they might have to
spend a night out on the open sea in the middle of a
Scottish winter, it also reflects the casual, half-hearted
approach to the hunt. The whalers wanted their holiday. The citizens of Dundee wanted a show. Remember
the chiding slight to the whalers in the newspaper
reports of the self-styled 'Eye Witness of the Chase':

> It naturally occurs to ordinary people to ask the question,
> Is this whale to be allowed to come up the river day after
> day in front of the good town of Dundee, and before the
> crews and captains of a dozen whalers, flaunt its tail and,
> figuratively speaking, put its flipper at its nose at them
> without a determined effort on their part to throw salt on
> its tail and lay it up on the beach, so that the general
> public may have a look at him?

The problem was identified late in the day, and by
Captain Yule, who before he left port in the *Iron King*

had arranged for a small steam vessel to take on necessary supplies and rendezvous with the convoy with as much haste as she could make. That turned out to be not very much haste at all. For although she did round up at least some supplies, it was Hogmanay, and then as now, Hogmanay is not the best day of the year in Scotland to stimulate the natives into urgency. And although the supply boat did sail eventually, she was overwhelmed by darkness, and of course she was carrying the spare lights that might have enabled her to find the convoy if the convoy had carried them in the first place. For whatever reason, she did not find the convoy, and returned to port with her cargo intact to find the city enthusiastically embracing the traditions of the New Year.

Meanwhile, somewhere between Bell Rock and Scurdy Ness, New Year came and went without fanfare, or even a raised glass – there was no glass to raise, and even if there had been, there was nothing to put in it. The optimism of early evening had ebbed inexorably as the whale swam on and on. The *Advertiser* narrated the denouement thus:

Early in the morning, however, a stiff easterly breeze sprang up, and a nasty sea rose, so that the strain on the line became very great. As daylight dawned, the prospects for capture were less hopeful, and with the view of accelerating death, a number of marlin-spikes and iron bolts were fired into its body, but without the desired effect. At half-past eight o'clock, when the tug was about four or five miles north-west of the Bell Rock, the line snapped within a few yards of the harpoon, and the fish, feeling itself free, swam vigorously away to the eastward. As nothing could be done to recapture it, owing to the want of gear, the tug and whaleboats returned to Dundee where they arrived about half past twelve o'clock . . .

. . . Although the fish seemed to swim away vigorously when it found itself free yesterday morning, it is the opinion of experienced whaling masters that it is not likely to survive its injuries, and that it may be picked up in a day or two. Three harpoons, having each a few fathoms of lines attached, were still in its body when it disappeared. Great crowds assembled at Dundee Harbour yesterday forenoon to learn the result of the chase, and much disappointment was felt when the news of failure became known. The whale is reported by those who had good opportunities of seeing it to be from 60–70 feet long . . .

(It is always the same with one-that-got-away stories – whatever the size of the one that got away, it is never quite big enough for those who let it slip from their grasp. The Tay Whale would prove to be 40 feet long.)

A single paragraph follow-up from the same newspaper later in the week added an astounding little postscript:

No trace of the wounded whale has yet been found. The opinion of those who were on board the steam tug *Iron King* is that it will be found dead in a day or two by the Broughty Ferry fishermen either when going to or returning from the fishing grounds. As yet, however, the fishermen have not been at sea. It is computed that the whale must have towed the steamer between 40 and 50 miles, and this is allowing a very small margin for the devious courses which it pursued. In addition, it pulled for six or seven miles the three heavy boats before those on board the steamer took the fish in hand. The *Iron King* is a heavy iron boat of considerable power, and it is calculated that the whale, from the time it was harpooned till it escaped – a period of 22 hours – swam over 50 miles, pulling a dead weight of between 20 and 30 tons nearly all the way.

Chapter 6

Death

With no enemies in the sea
The whale is loth to believe in the attack
As were the Indians, as were the aborigines.

The Nootka claim that the whale allows his death,
To spare people from hunger
And that therefore they must be worthy of it.

Heathcote Williams
Whale Nation, 1988

The whale shed its burden as dawn broke on the New Year of 1884. It had felt the burden begin to weaken, to grow more unwieldy as the line began to give. It twisted its body left and right, arched its back, rose and fell, saw the waves grow tall and quicken so that the boats and even the Bell Rock Lighthouse disappeared for several seconds at a time. It knew that sea-change for an ally, felt encouragement, summoned all the energy that was left. It did not occur to the whale that what was left might not be enough. But it knew the boats swam less fluently in big seas, knew too that the big seas did not affect the light one way or the other, that it remained the lowest star in the night sky, that it flashed more brightly than the other stars, that it also made light like moonbeams, and these the whale understood.

It seized on the memory of countless mid-ocean nights when it would lie perfectly still on the surface at the centre of its circular world (the ocean horizon unbroken through 360 degrees, the dome of the sky, the rounded depths of ocean), at the centre of the rhythmic cycles that played there – moon, stars and shooting stars, the south-in-autumn-north-in-spring rituals of geese and swans, the haphazard dance of the aurora borealis. All these had underpinned its life, regular as tides, until this last ebb.

The whale might have let go then, might have died there, still tethered to the source of its suffering, close to the lowest star in the sky that made the light like moonbeams, and with the beauty of that oceanic memory painted on its mind's eye. But that is not the way with great whales. The remembering had calmed the whale again and dulled its suffering and instilled the illusion of returning strength. The sea hammered over it suddenly, and James Lyons's harpoon twisted deeper, and pain seared in steel shafts. The moonbeams snuffed out (the Bell Rock light extinguished for the day), and the whale was fighting for its life again in the grey dawn of the North Sea, and it heaved again, and it felt again the tethering line weaken.

So James Lyons's God did not let the whale die quickly. After twenty-two hours it was still swimming. Twenty-two hours after Lyons harpooned it from the steam launch of the *Polar Star* and saw his harpoon strike true and bite deep and hold fast, and urged his notion of God to let the whale die quickly, it still lived. Twenty-two hours in which it suffered two more harpoon strikes, twenty-two hours in which all manner of iron missiles had peppered its flanks as liberally as buckshot (and how many bullets and sundry varieties of improvised ammunition were fired into it in the previous six weeks by amateurs and idiots playing games with guns in open boats is anyone's guess), twenty-two hours in which it had hauled first the steam launch then the two open whale boats, one of which was replaced by the brute mass of the *Iron King*, hauled them all from the narrows of the firth to the open sea, where the Bell Rock brightened the long winter darkness for perhaps eighteen of the twenty-two hours . . . after all that, the harpoonist's God had declined to let the whale die.

And in any case it had declined to die itself, and then it was the last harpoon line and then the whalers that gave up the ghost.

The whalers were defeated. They were defeated not just by their own half-heartedness but because they underestimated and misunderstood the wildness that was in the whale's blood. They were defeated by its wild resolve; by the wild strength that was the servant of its resolve; by the wild power that it could bring to bear in controlled spasms; by the wild knowledge that it leaned on and wedded to the sea's increasingly turbulent mood. 'Owing to the heavy strain caused by the breeze the remaining line, being nearly worn through, broke,' wrote the anonymous pamphleteer of 1884, 'and the whale swam away out to sea, carrying with it enough of the war material of its foes to start a small museum.' It would do better than that in the years to come, but its museum career was still ahead of it.

It 'sped on to Stonehaven with all its might', wrote McGonagall, flourishing his poetic licence deep within the bounds of his ignorance, but in truth it did nothing of the kind. True, it would have surged forward when it felt the burden fall away, and in the whaleboats that was their last sight of it alive, and that was the story they would take back to port with them – the whale sped away. But the debilitating effects of blood-loss and pain and exhaustion had accumulated beyond all prospect of recovery. The whale was beyond speeding; all the resources it could muster were sufficient only to allow it to vanish from the sight of the weary pursuers. Freedom, when it finally came, was too late. The whale was too damaged. The wildness was in it like blood, but its blood was strewn back down the open sea for 50 miles. It was free, but only to dive deep, free to die alone, free to die untethered. Yet as long as the last residues of wildness sustained the whale, it swam. It swam unerringly north, thinking only of life and living, for north was where the open ocean lay, and the northern ocean was sanctuary, sanctuary and life and living. And because of the boats at the surface, and because it did not know that it had outlasted them and that they had given up, it dived deep, and the deep sea opened to it and comforted it.

The whale dived on a single intake of breath, and as it dived deeper it allowed its chest to collapse, which is the whale's way of handling the enormous pressure of deep-sea diving. The lungs collapse at about 300 feet down; any remaining air is held in the windpipe and nasal passages, and nitrogen, which produces problems like 'the bends' for human divers, cannot be absorbed. And then the whale can dive and dive and dive, sustained by oxygen in its tissues, and stay deep for well over an hour at perhaps 10,000 feet down. All this exerts extraordinary pressures on the whale, but the whale is extraordinarily fashioned to cope with it. One of the earliest scientific accounts of whaling in the northern oceans, written by William Scoresby in 1820, made the following calculations:

The surface of the body of a large whale may be considered as comprising an area of 1540 square feet. This, under the common weight of the atmosphere only, must sustain a pressure of 1386 tons. But at the depth of 800 fathoms [4800 feet], where there is a column of water equal in weight to about 154 atmospheres, the pressure on the animals must be equal to 211,200 tons. This is a degree of pressure of which we can have but an imperfect conception. It may assist our comprehension, however, to be informed that it exceeds in weight sixty of the largest ships of the British Navy, when manned, provisioned, and fitted for a six-month cruise.

I confess my conception remains imperfect, but I have the gist of it.

So the whale dived deep, and as it dived the sense of tranquillity also deepened. The whale wanted a reef to rasp against, to wrench the harpoons from its body. It wanted to open the harpoon wounds to the benevolent sea. It intended to survive. There were no enemies in the sea below the surface. There was no reason to fear. And if it proved too difficult to get back to the surface, it would find and summon other whales and these would come to its aid. It would call for help. Perhaps it had been calling since the first harpoon bit and held and the whale felt the sudden drag of the first boat.

It is not a fanciful notion. The copious literature of whaling over more than 200 years – and more recently of nature writing about the whales themselves – is awash with accounts of whales going to the aid of their own kind. Lyall Watson and Tom Ritchie in *Whales of the World* (1981) wrote that 'most, if not all whale species have a powerful, possibly innate, tendency to come to the aid of others in distress. And it is entirely appropriate that this behaviour pattern should involve the simple invariable response of helping an ailing animal to get to the surface. One of the stimuli which sparks the response seems to be a distress call.'

An injured whale's cry for help is so effective that the early whalers (in the days before the explosive harpoon was invented) relied on a whale they had already harpooned to lure others within shooting range, and killed many whales that way. Strange that the rescuer-whales never learned to suspect a trap, although of course there must be many occasions when the whale's distress is not caused by whalers. But the impulse to rescue was known to galvanise loitering whales or prompt a change of course in swimming whales several miles away. There is also this: the lowest 'notes' in the astonishing repertoire of humpback 'songs' can travel hundreds and perhaps thousands of miles through water to be received by other humpbacks. Their meanings baffle science, a state of affairs I find profoundly reassuring. My heart leaps with gratitude every time some workaday function of nature confounds the best efforts of smart-ass science. And science is baffled by almost every aspect of whale song, not least by the fact that whales don't open their mouths to sing, nor is it clear which part of their bodies is the singing part. But what science does know, because it has been observed time without number, is that a whale in distress can send out a cry for help. One possible conclusion to draw from all this is that humpbacks, the most accomplished singers among whales, are capable of mobilising rescue parties from far beyond the horizon.

But there is no evidence to suggest that there was a rescue mission for the Tay Whale. It was an adolescent male making its way in the world, sometimes in the company of other humpbacks, sometimes alone, which is how humpbacks travel, and it seems that it was more or less lost. Humpbacks do not normally linger within the force field of the Tay estuary. There were probably none closer to the Tay Whale when it died than the North Atlantic off Norway, and the North Atlantic off Norway is probably where the Tay Whale took the first of two fatal wrong turnings. (The second was to turn right at the Bell Rock.)

If it had sounded its first distress call when the first harpoon struck and held and the drag of the steam launch from the *Polar Star* kicked in, and if it had carried on calling for more than 24 hours as its difficulties increased, there would have been all the information 'out there' that a rescue party might need. These calls would have travelled through the North Sea at a mile a second, five times faster than through the air, and they would have been more than capable of travelling as far as Norway. Science theorises that whales many thousands of miles apart travel towards each other to mate, and find each other by calling, even though they may have to swim for weeks before they meet. That leaves me free to theorise that a rescue mission might have set out on a similar journey, to come to the aid of the Tay Whale, but that it turned back when the Tay Whale stopped calling because it died, and that the huge brains of whales allowed the rescue party to conclude that its journey was fruitless.

The Tay Whale was on its own. It dived deep, it found a reef on which it wrenched two of the three harpoons from its body and then it began to die alone.

In the endless roll-call of all the sorry, inglorious thousands of deaths that the whaling industry has ever inflicted on the tribe of whales anywhere and everywhere in all the oceans of the world, there was surely never a more inexcusable and pointless death than this one. I am with Thoreau on the matter of killing whales: 'Can he who has discovered only some of the uses of whale-bone and whale oil be said to have discovered the true use of the whale? Can he who slays the elephant for its ivory be said to have seen the elephant? These are petty and accidental uses; just as if a stronger race were to kill us in order to make buttons and flageolets of our bones . . .'

The killing of a whale to make do with its 'petty and accidental uses' is grim enough. The killing of a whale for no reason at all, other than that it turned up where it did and the people in the place where it turned up knew how to kill it . . . that is a touch grimmer. Knowledge of the details merely piles on the culpability. This was a young whale that might have lived to be 200 and sired flotillas of whales; to kill it half-heartedly and in *that* way, the job botched so badly that the whale suffered all the eternities of agonies that any dying whale can ever suffer . . . that is savagery. And it all happened in the place on the map that I call home, my own ancestors were surely among the cheering, laughing mobs, the descendants of the whalers themselves are in the streets where I am accustomed to walk. For a nature writer, that is not an easy inheritance to be handed.

Time airbrushed away the details of the story. The city laughed at it through the eyes of McGonagall, who credited God with the whole thing, so that's all right then. But writing down the whale's death and growing angry has made it acutely personal for me. It was not all right, and McGonagall's faintly mocking tone only reflected the prevailing mood of the time and the place. The city was as culpable as the whalers.

To choose to write it down, knowing in advance how my home city comes out of the story, is like firing an explosive harpoon into the exposed flank of its reputation among the seagoing places of the world. Without apology, I take aim and fire. And I hope she feels it.

Chapter 7

Capture

And was first seen by the crew of a Gourdon fishing boat,
Which they thought was a big coble upturned afloat;
But when they drew near they saw it was a whale,
So they resolved to tow it ashore without fail.

So they got a rope from each boat tied round his tail,
And landed their burden at Stonehaven without fail;
And when the people saw it their voices they did raise,
Declaring that the brave fishermen deserved great praise.

And my opinion is that God sent the whale in time of need,
No matter what other people may think or what is their creed;
I know fishermen in general are often very poor,
And God in His goodness sent it to drive poverty from their door.

William McGonagall
'The Famous Tay Whale'

The whale vanished for a week. During the night after
it escaped from the boats, it died on the bottom of the
North Sea. When it was next seen on the morning of 7
January 1884, it was floating upside-down on the surface and its bloated white belly was being ripped open
by hordes of gulls. Before it died it had bled for the

better part of two days; no, the worse part. As it weakened, as whale-life became a one-way tide on its final ebb, the muscles around its ribs that facilitated breathing became enfeebled. Air valves collapsed. The sea poured in and flooded its lungs. It suffocated. It rolled over and over, a supreme swimmer of the world's oceans, both nimble sprinter and long-haul ocean-to-ocean pilgrim, rendered helpless and limp in the utter blackness of the deep; and ultimately, slowly, wearily beyond anything it had ever known, dead. And God had nothing to do with it.

There were no witnesses to the death of the Tay Whale. There is nothing to be seen at such a depth. In exceptional circumstances, none of them in the North Sea but rather in the lyrical tropical waters of the world's most seductive travel brochures, visibility near the surface is around 100 feet. The longest underwater distance ever recorded by human sight is about 1,000 feet but that was in the utterly still sea-water under shore-fast Antarctic ice. One hundred feet down in the North Sea even on a sunny summer's day at high noon, a whale would be unable to see its own tail. Indeed, for much of its underwater life, a whale inhabits a realm too murky to see its own tail. At the bottom of the North Sea, and for that matter, anywhere below a depth of about 50 feet on a grey January morning, the Tay Whale saw nothing at all, but rather used its voice and the underwater landscape to navigate by sonar. Such a whale sings its way round the world. By the time it was seen again it had sung its last, and in seven days it had barely travelled 20 miles north of what it had come to know as the lowest star in its sky.

Currents and tides had drifted it along the sea bottom, but as it bloated with water it began inexorably to lift. The sea, having reclaimed it and nurtured its last hours, then deposited it upside-down on the surface where the sun shone on its upturned white belly, an invitation for every seabird within 50 square miles to home in on a magnificent feast. So it was that when the crew of a fishing boat from the tiny Kincardineshire village of Gourdon first sighted a horde of gulls hovering and diving down on what appeared to be the overturned hull of a boat, they gave the thing a long, hard look. The boat was ten miles south-east of Gourdon, and the birds a further five miles out. The crew buoyed their lines and made what speed they could with sail and oars. They found not a wreck but the wreckage of the whale, deduced that this was *the* Tay Whale, or the Dundee Whale as that coast had come to know it as its fame spread. Whatever they called it, they recognised a windfall when they saw one, and decided to try and cash in. Their share in a dead whale, if they could land it, would amount to rather more than a day's herring fishing. From the standpoint of the twenty-first century, you might think the indignity that the whale had already suffered was quite enough. You might think some spasm of conscience would afflict the collective seafaring mind of that coast. After all, it had died hideously, and now, if it was left to nature to dispose of one of its own, it was about to be shredded by the creatures of the sea. But McGonagall's God had other ideas. The crew put about and headed back to port, where one of their number was despatched with all haste to Montrose to secure the services of a tug. Why they chose to make for Gourdon rather than directly for Montrose is not explained, for the distance was almost identical, but it proved to be both a costly and an embarrassing mistake. In everything that followed, the name of that particular boat is the only one that has not survived, as though some benevolent conspiracy of silence had been agreed to mask the crew's distress. The whale, meanwhile, was about to embark on its long, long afterlife.

The crewman who had been despatched to cover the ten landward miles to Montrose with what haste he could muster (presumably a fast horse, or at least the fastest one that was at the disposal of a small-time fisherman), would have done well to swear his fellow crewmen to silence for the duration of his mission. As it was, they succumbed to the temptation to brag about their good fortune, and how they planned to cash in on it. They blabbed. And before you could say Moby Dick, three more Gourdon fishing boats, the *Esquimaux*, the *Esk* and the *Guiding Star*, were mobilised, fully crewed and making line-astern for the whale's last known position, while the crew of the unsung boat that found it in the first place were a man short and waiting for a tug from Montrose.

By noon the three fishing boats had the carcase surrounded, and their skippers were stroking their chins. Less than half the whale was visible above the water, and they must have wondered briefly at least whether signing up to the services of the Montrose tug might have been a better option. The two problems: how to get a line, or rather three lines, round the whale to make it fast to the three boats; and having secured its brute mass, how to get it home. The difficulty with the first problem was that it couldn't be solved without putting men onto the whale, which was not without obvious risks. The difficulty with the second was coordinating the progress of three fishing boats powered by sail and oars, given that communication among the ships would be by shouting and that most of the journey with the whale in tow would be undertaken in darkness. At least the Gourdon boats had lights.

So each boat put a man on the whale, and each got a line round the tail, then reinforced the connection with a long chain from one of the boats, which was kept slack in case any of the lines broke. Enter the *Storm King*, the Montrose steam tug, ever so slightly late, complete with the crewman from the Gourdon boat that had found the whale. You can imagine how he was feeling at the sight

70

that greeted his eyes as the tug closed in on the whale. The skipper of the tug offered his assistance, more in hope than in expectation, but the Gourdon boats were in a position of strength and politely declined. As the anonymous pamphleteer put it (with a hefty dose of the sardonic that characterised almost every single report of the event, whatever the journal): 'the captors, with a view to the conservation of possible profits, determined to make an effort to land their fish unassisted, arranging with the captain of the *Storm King* that, if through stress of weather they had to part with their prize, they would telegraph him from whatever port they might land at as to where they had had "to let go their painter".'

So with the *Esquimaux* leading and towing dead ahead of the whale, and the *Esk* and the *Guiding Star* either side and slightly ahead of the whale (and with a rope between them which was also passed over the whale), the unwieldy convoy set off for distant Gourdon, assisted by a wind from the west-south-west. Even with four or five oars on each boat, the labour was colossal. If the wind had held, they might have made Gourdon by midnight, had a dram or two to celebrate their adventure and slept gloriously in their own beds. But remember McGonagall's God was orchestrating the deal, and had mischief on his mind. The wind backed into the north. The fishermen conferred and changed course for Montrose, although doubtless they were less than confident of the reception they would receive there, given that they had snubbed the skipper of the *Storm King*. Whether that was what was preying on their minds, or whether the wind changed again, they were still seven or eight miles out from Montrose when they decided that their best bet (which presumably meant the best 'conservation of possible profits') was to run for Stonehaven instead.

They no more 'ran' for Stonehaven than the Tay Whale 'sped on to Stonehaven with all his might' in McGonagall's phrase. Their progress was more akin to crawling on all fours than running. One of the oarsmen summed up the journey in the cold light of day: 'It was an awfu' job.'

They were still rowing at daybreak, which would be about 8 a.m., and 20 hours after they had secured the whale, and they must have covered 30 miles with the whale in tow, but they were hugely encouraged by the sight of Stonehaven's near neighbour Dunnottar Castle on its clifftop, which meant they were almost high and dry and with their prize intact. The tide was high, and the boats landed the whale without difficulty, and in keeping with what had already become a tradition whenever the Tay Whale was centre stage, the town had come out to stand and stare. The town bellman had been despatched to spread the word, and the crowd grew as the tide ebbed, and the full impact of what it was the Gourdon boats had landed was slowly revealed. It also changed shape, from its bloated condition to something more whale-shaped as the sea-water began to pour out of it. And, as it had been landed upside-down, there was the further transformation and a great 'Oooooooohhhhh!' from the crowd once the whale had been righted and they saw the one remaining harpoon still embedded there with a few feet of frayed line.

There was something about that potent image – the massive death of the ocean-dweller, the flimsy symbol of the land-dweller that pursues the whale to the ends of the earth. A philosopher among the crowd might have paused to weigh the immensity of that ancient conflict of species, the pacifist whale against the warrior whaler, and wonder if it was all worth it. To land this whale, a youngster, little more than a child-whale, on the Stonehaven shingle had taken eight days, the whale had towed first four boats then three for 50 miles, and having escaped and vanished and died and resurfaced a week later, the whale itself had been hauled in death for 30 miles. In Dundee, the hunt for the living whale had involved a steam launch, two open whalers, the harbour tug and a supply boat that never supplied anything, and upwards of twenty crewmen. In Gourdon, the attempt to secure the dead whale had involved four different fishing boats and the Montrose tug, upwards of twenty more crewmen, so almost fifty in total. The end result was this huge ugliness on the shore at Stonehaven, and a deal with an entrepreneur whose identity is lost now which netted the crews of the *Esquimaux,* the *Esk* and the *Guiding Star* £10 a head. In 1884, it would have taken them weeks to put £10 in their pockets. McGonagall was right in their eyes, a God-given pay day, but it is a strange species of God that permits such a wondrous creation as a humpback whale to die in such a fashion so that the creature He made in His own image can enjoy the mother and father of all hangovers. You can be sure Gourdon was drunk for a week.

Gourdon, January 2008, 125 years after the event, was shivering. A wind blew in from Norway and it smelled of snow, but an east coast sun flayed the waves and bounced viciously off the water into the eyes of the village. The places crouches in level tiers along its low hillside, crouches round its double harbour. The burial ground is on its highest edge. Land down by the harbour is much too valuable to squander on the dead. Even the last journey of the villagers is an uphill struggle: funerals climb Brae Road. No one wasted much time or imagination on choosing a name for Gourdon's main thoroughfare. After the graveyard, the school, then the steepening downhill and the inevitable hairpin at the foot, the unfailing pattern of east-coast fishing villages from Caithness to the Border; there was always a cliff to negotiate. I parked by the harbour, feeling very conspicuous. I watched out for blown tumbleweed.

The village looked empty. The feeling was quite

different from a village where the net curtains twitch and you know you are being watched. Here, it felt like there was no one behind the curtains to twitch them. The air smelled agreeably of salt air and fish.

A man in a long coat and a warm hat passed by on the other side of the road without looking my way. I walked out along one side of the harbour making a mental note of boat names, a game I have played since childhood, though I have never owned a boat. I just like to read boat names. I liked *Vivid* and *Sine Bhan* (an odd Gaelic note in such an un-Gaelic part of Scotland; it means Fair Sheena (or Jean), and it is also the title of the kind of pipe tune that in the hands of the right kind of piper melts the coldest heart and makes strong men weep). The *Harvester* was in from Aberdeen. The *Ellen*-something or other (I forget, I was making mental notes, it was too cold for writing anything down) lay across the harbour and looked like the most serious trawler in port. I walked round to have a look her, ran the eye of a maritime incompetent over her, liked the cut of her jib (not that she had a jib, but if she had, I would have liked its cut). All the way round, the quayside was paved with broken bits of lobster that crunched beneath my feet, and every yard of harbour wall had its gull, waiting, waiting, making belligerent eye contact, each opened throat crying: 'Gimme!'

I turned back after my inspection of the *Ellen*-something-or-other, to find the man in the long coat and the warm hat bearing down. I suspected that he was looking for conversation and that he thought he had found a soft target.

'It's a bonnie morning,' I offered.

'Bitter, bitter wind,' he said. It was bitter, bitter.

'Aye, but you've got sunshine. It's snowing all the way west of Brechin to the Atlantic.' It was. I'd just driven that bit to get here. He seemed not to hear.

'The fishing's in a terrible state.' It seems he had seen me inspecting the trawler. 'No money in it. And the people won't buy fresh fish. Too expensive.'

'How many boats left in Gourdon?'

'Fishing boats? Three or four. It's the worst it's ever been in my lifetime. I've never known it so bad.'

'Is this your place?'

'Oh yes. I go back 400 years here.'

So I told him he was the man I wanted to talk to. I was writing about the Tay Whale and wondered about the Gourdon lads who plucked its carcase from the sea.

'I don't know about that,' he said, vaguely annoyed with himself that he had failed to answer a visitor's question. He struck me as one who was accustomed to countering visitors' questions with satisfactory answers.

'Was that near here?'

'About 15 miles out, south-east,' I said. 'They were Gourdon boats.'

He searched his memory, shook his head.

'I didn't know that. They boiled a whale in that

building over there, early in the twentieth century. It was very controversial. And there was the stench of it, and that area was so crowded then.'

But he had provided illumination, unwitting illumination, but illumination for all that. He had made me aware in that instant of the Gourdon fishermen's take on the Tay Whale. It was just another fish. It was just another bloody fish in . . . ('The village was founded in 1350 . . .') . . . thank you, in 750 years of catching fish.

'You see the white tower up the hill?'

White tower? He pointed. Ah, the faded white tower, the height of a house, round and conically capped, hardly visible in the press of houses if you didn't know where to look. It was not always thus.

'And do you see the white patch on the wall with the red thing?'

It was the back wall of the harbour, a tall, white-washed oblong with a red lifebelt housing halfway up. It looked nothing like the white tower, but it used to.

'Navigation lights. That was where the lower one stood. They demolished it.' I guessed he did not approve of 'they' who demolished it. 'I don't know if you are aware of this but there is a very treacherous reef out there.' He gestured vaguely beyond the harbour wall. 'You lined up the two towers, the one above the other, and that was your line in.' And at night, of course, the towers would have been lit. But the lights have gone out in Gourdon.

I wasn't sure what I would find in Gourdon in the midwinter of 2008, but the last thing I expected to feel was a pang of sympathy. The reason for the village's very existence is pretty well extinct. Oh, there are still fish in the North Sea, but the advent of factory ships, EU quotas and the remoteness of the lawmakers inevitably legislates against the little guys. A fishing fleet of three or four boats is only going one way, and sooner or later it will sink without trace to become a footnote in a fisheries museum.

Its story is all too commonplace along the fishing coasts of the northern hemisphere: a small community is founded on a single idea – catching fish (and servicing the needs of the men who catch fish – building and repairing boats, building up the natural harbour that had turned the heads of the original villagers in the first place) and catching more fish. At Gourdon, it went well enough for the first 600 years or so, gloriously through the nineteenth-century herring boom, but it has dwindled down these last few decades to this last low ebb. It would be cold comfort to the man in the long coat and the warm hat to argue that it is a good idea that endures for 600 years, for his father had been a fisherman and I am compelled to imagine that the previous 300 years of his family's tenure before his father were spent fishing too. He was the notable exception to his own rule, and had become a teacher, but that conspicuous exception apart, what else are you going to do in Gourdon that keeps you there for 400 years?

I got the impression, standing listening to him, that community life in Gourdon had gone the way of the Tay Whale, and was now floating belly up, still afloat, but more or less dead, with an unappetising future as a museum piece. The community, he said, had been inundated by 'strangers', which proved to be a euphemism for the English. They are your neighbours, he said, but you never see them. They leave early in the morning to work in Aberdeen and they come home late and lock the doors. They play no part in the community. In the days when three boats from Gourdon's teeming fleet usurped their comrades' find and 'captured' the dead whale, you worked where you lived, and you would no more lock your door than give up fishing and try planting barley on the beach.

And there were five pubs and 'dram houses'. 'Do you know what dram houses were?' he asked. I nodded and smiled. He did not return my smile. 'Oh, it was an awful drunken trade,' he said, and I wondered, without daring to ask, if that was what had stopped him going to the fishing himself.

Incredibly, it seems now, the railway came here too, burrowing in under the cliffs in the late nineteenth century, until Dr Beeching swung his infamous axe in the late 1960s. The railways were a good idea too, but their heyday was a little shorter-lived than Gourdon's.

The big walls on the seaward side of the brae mark the uppermost extent of the railway company's empire. It might only have been Gourdon, but they still felt it necessary to proclaim themselves in high stone walls.

It's all gone. What has replaced it looks well enough to a casual by-passer's eye, the sea-facing buildings are mostly well-wrought, traditionally styled and clad in east-coast harling, the allure of the harbour, a view that encompasses 50 square miles of sun-smitten sea, and a sky that reaches all the way to Norway in the north, to Holland in the east, at least to Dundee in the south, and that way (the cramped, landward side) . . . who cares? But it's too clean, too orderly, for a working fishing village, and yes, it's too empty.

We had walked back along the pier, and paused as our ways parted. I said I had enjoyed talking to the man in the long coat and the warm hat. He said thank you so much, and walked off without a backward glance. I drove back up out of the village and onto the main road, and stopped again at once in a lay-by high above the harbour.

You can see the whole village from there, see how it funnels towards the harbour, and beyond the harbour you can see the whole of the Tay Whale's last living journey. That far hint of blue headland is north Fife, that skyline smudge is the Bell Rock lighthouse, and somewhere out there to the south-east, in the midst of that tract of sea, the unnamed Gourdon boat found the whale, determined to profit by it, and sent for a tug and had the whale stolen from under her nose by her own kind.

And surely they were all-but-blameless opportunists in the matter of the Tay Whale? (I imagine the great-grandfather of the man in the long coat and the warm hat standing on the carcase in the sea, cheerfully in his element as he wrestled with the rope and the whale's tail.) They probably agreed with McGonagall – it was God's gift. What they made of it – £10 a man – was an exceptional windfall for a day's work. And whether each scattered it around the community's needy as hard cash or in largesse distributed in the dram houses and inns, it would permeate Gourdon's lifeblood one way or the other.

And it was just one more fish, wasn't it?

And they were all-but-blameless, weren't they?

And it was already dead and done-for, the dirty work of their big-city comrades down the coast, wasn't it?

Yes, and yes, and yes.

And yet, and yet . . .

. . . By their actions, the Gourdon fishermen made it possible for the Tay Whale to be exploited for the next 125 years, a process that goes on unabated. As I write this, the McManus Galleries and Museum in Dundee is undergoing a major refurbishment. When it re-opens, the skeleton of the Tay Whale will be the centrepiece of a new whaling exhibit. For the moment, it is being stored in several pieces in various buildings in the city. If they have trouble reassembling the skeleton when the time comes, it won't be the first time. You can be sure, too, that McGonagall's poem will feature in the display and that will diminish in many people's eyes the hideous nature of what befell the whale, first at the hands of the Dundee whalers, then at the hands of the Gourdon fishermen. You cannot blame them for McGonagall (no one can satisfactorily account for McGonagall's status in his adopted city and far beyond for that matter), but they harnessed the whale to their boats and, by their own Herculean labours, landed it at Stonehaven, then they made a transaction that made an auction possible, that made a freak show possible, that made a public humiliation of the whale possible and eventually a museum exhibit for 125 years, and all that time, the same whale could have been swimming the world's oceans, singing.

The Dundee whalers killed it. The Gourdon fishermen ensured, albeit unwittingly, that it would be disembowelled, stuffed, stitched up and paraded, that its tongue would fall out into the docks at Dundee, that its heart would fill a large barrel . . . and that a Dundee-born child would have his dreams tormented by the skeleton, and that the same child, having grown and become a journalist and then a nature writer who once eye-balled a humpback whale in Alaska and looked down into its blowhole from a few feet above and heard it sing, would take the death and subsequent diminution of the Tay Whale's life very, very personally. And so I do.

I feel for what the Gourdons of my country have become, for the demise of local traditions and local character and community individuality. These are all regrettable wherever in the world they occur. And Gourdon sticks in my craw too. But Dundee is my place on the map, and if Dundee had not inflicted its pointless viciousness on the whale, and just let it come and go and delighted in its presence, Gourdon would never have been part of the story.

An ambassador of the tribe of whales (a tribe millions of years old, a tribe alongside whom the dinosaurs were a race of sticklebacks) paid a call in my home river. My home town responded with exploding harpoons. To them it was a whale all right, and they had a great awareness of the character and nobility and beauty of the animal as well as its commercial worth, but to the Gourdon crews, it was just one more bloody fish.

But back in the city of my birth, the progress-in-death of the Tay Whale was being stalked every inch of the way by the kind of maverick industrialist with a taste for show business that no fiction writer would dare to invent. The show was far from over. It was about to go on and on and on.

Chapter 8

Greasy Johnny

The mighty whale doth in these harbours lye,
Whose oyl the careful merchant deare will buy.

William Morrell
New England, 1625

So Mr John Wood has bought it for two hundred
   and twenty-six pound,
And has brought it to Dundee all safe and all sound;
Which measures 40 feet in length from the snout
   to the tail,
So I advise the people far and near to see it without
   fail.

William McGonagall
'The Famous Tay Whale'

Ah me! How the old celebrities of Dundee do move off to the silent land! Here is now John Woods, of Tay Whale fame, gathered to his fathers. John then achieved a celebrity he never would have had but for his purchase of the playful finner which exactly 12 years ago this month was disporting itself in the shallows of our noble river.

An ordinary whale would have been little to its proprietor. But this whale had been the talk of the town and district for months. Its capture after many

Dangling from a 70-ton steam crane, the carcase of the Tay Whale is lifted ashore by the light of a full moon at Dundee docks. Huge crowds gathered although it was well after midnight in early January. The whale's tongued lolled out of its mouth then fell into the water. Divers recovered it the following day. *McManus Galleries and Museum, Dundee.*

The Tay Whale lies upside down on the shore at Stonehaven. Three fishing boats from nearby Gourdon had towed it there having come across the carcase floating on the surface of the sea a week after it had been harpooned by Dundee whalers. The whale had escaped but with fatal injuries. *McManus Galleries and Museum, Dundee.*

One small dog and the inevitable crowd of people try to make sense of the arrival of a dead humpback whale on the shore at Stonehaven. The carcase was auctioned there and bought for £226 by Dundee oil merchant John Woods who immediately arranged for it to be towed back to Dundee by a tugboat. *McManus Galleries and Museum, Dundee.*

Above. The Tay Whale at the Woods oil yard in Dundee. Visitors posed in the propped-up mouth to have their photographs taken. A best-selling postcard superimposed this shot of the whale on a different background – a sunset over the Tay! *McManus Galleries and Museum, Dundee.*

Below. The whale's carcase was partially dissected and embalmed at the Woods yard by Professor John Struthers of Aberdeen University; much of its skeleton was removed and replaced by a wooden frame, and its flesh and vital organs were replaced by a stuffing of straw. It was in this guise that the whale went on a nationwide tour by rail. *McManus Galleries and Museum, Dundee.*

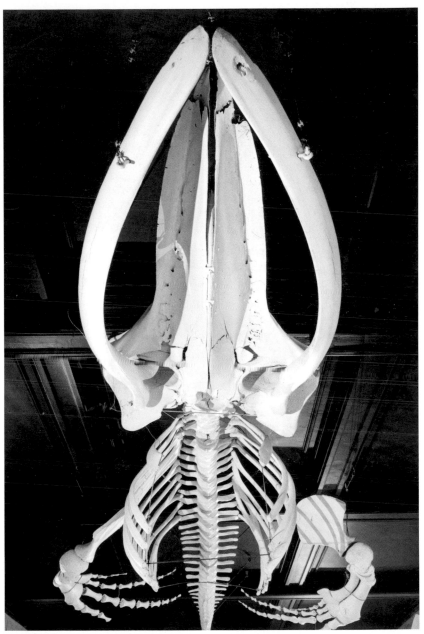

The skeleton of the Tay Whale was eventually presented by John Woods to the city of Dundee, despite lucrative offers from big museums in London, Europe and America. It has been on display in the city's principal museum more or less ever since. *McManus Galleries and Museum, Dundee.*

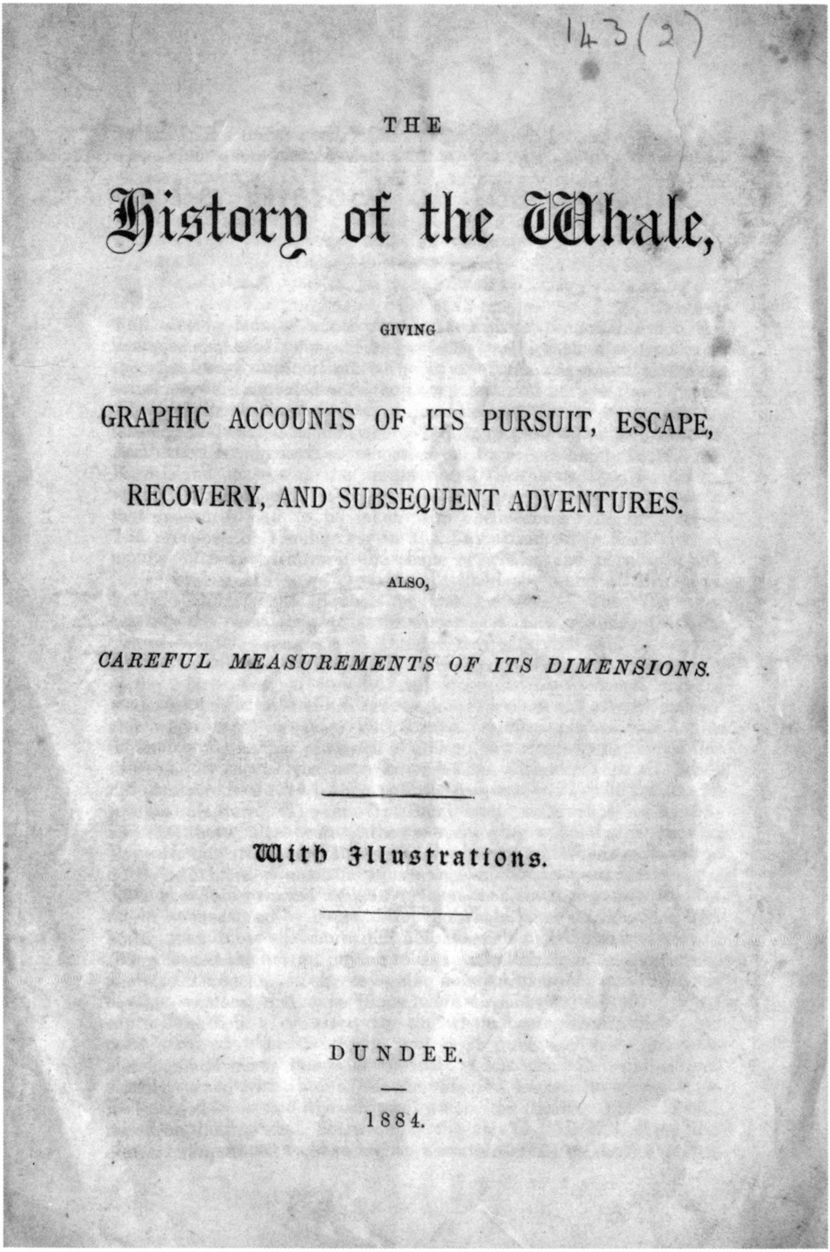

THE

History of the Whale,

GIVING

GRAPHIC ACCOUNTS OF ITS PURSUIT, ESCAPE,

RECOVERY, AND SUBSEQUENT ADVENTURES.

ALSO,

CAREFUL MEASUREMENTS OF ITS DIMENSIONS.

———

With Illustrations.

———

DUNDEE.
—
1884.

A booklet detailing the story of the whale's arrival in the Tay, 'its pursuit, escape, recovery and subsequent adventures'. Note that the word 'death' does not appear on the title page, and the word 'recovery' is ambiguous to say the least. It was the whale's corpse that was recovered. *Scran.*

PROVISIONAL PROGRAMME.

In GREAT HALL, at 7.30,

LORD PROVOST MATHEWSON

WILL GIVE AN INTRODUCTORY ADDRESS.

CONCERT
OF
VOCAL AND INSTRUMENTAL MUSIC.

LECTURES.

In the EAST ROOM of the MUSEUM, at 8.30.

Professor Struthers, M.D., F.R.S.,

On "The Skeleton of the Tay Whale."

In the SCULPTURE GALLERY, at 9 o'clock,

Principal Peterson, M.A., LL.D.,

On "Ancient Sculpture,"

(Illustrated by the Casts in the City Museum.)

In the GREAT HALL, at 9.30,

Professor A. M. Paterson, M.D.,

On "Facial Expression,"

(Illustrated by Models and Diagrams.)

CONCERT.

In 1891, Dundee Naturalists Society hosted a grandly title 'Conversazione' – a social meeting devoted to the arts or sciences. The programme indicates a lecture by Professor Struthers on 'The Skeleton of the Tay Whale'. Seven years after the event, it seems, the professor was still making money out of the Tay Whale. *Scran.*

This extraordinary cartoon of 1885 shows Professor Struthers indulging his passion for whales – dissecting dead ones, that is. The whale on which the professor sits is thought to be a rare beluga which he is known to have acquired. The canister by the whale's mouth, the effects of which it is apparently enjoying, contains chloroform. *Scran.*

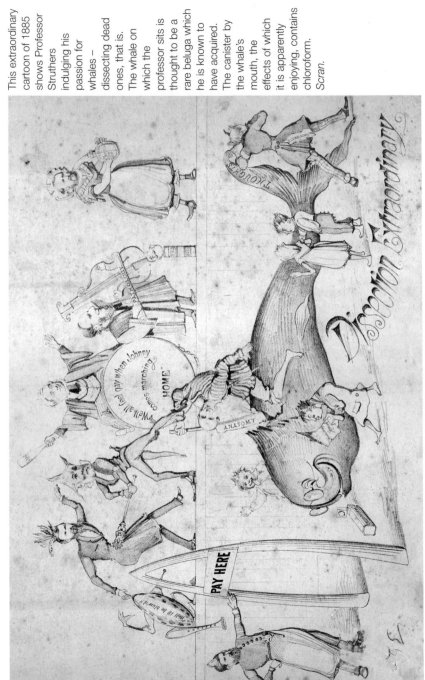

abortive attempts, its exhibition over the country, its dissection by Professor Struthers at Aberdeen University, and the presentation of its skeleton to our local museum, made the gigantic cetacean and its owner famous.

John was a character in his way. He was not unknown in our local courts, where the authorities had a word to say to him regarding the scents and odours of his oil factory, designated by the unsympathetic authorities by the hard and unpoetic name of nuisances.

But these I would not parade to the prejudice of the departed. I would rather ask his compatriots to think of the whale, and to go and visit the anatomy of the monster mammal in its resting place in the Albert Institute, and there shed a tear to the donor's memory.

Obituary in *The Piper o' Dundee*
December 1895

The Death occurred this week at Woods Cottage, East Dock Street, of Mr John Woods. Deceased, who was 66 years of age was best known in Dundee and throughout the country on account of his connection with the Tay Whale . . . Mr Woods, who has carried on the business of an oil merchant for a number of years, was at one time interested in the old Seagate Theatre. He was married three times.

Obituary in *The Courier*
November 1895

The memory of John Woods has fared less well than his star attraction these last 125 years. I suppose a name-check in a McGonagall poem is immortality of a kind, even a misspelled name-check, but whereas the whale has lived on in death as a more-or-less permanent exhibition showpiece, John Woods vanished with that less-than-heartfelt obituary in the irreverent (and now long extinct) weekly journal, *The Piper o' Dundee*, and a handful of lines in *The Courier*, Dundee's still vigorous daily newspaper. But he was, you can be sure, among the crowds that thronged the riverside vantage points when the whale was strutting its stuff in the Tay. He liked stuff-strutters. He was one himself. He was short and dark and tending towards stoutness, thanks to what some say was an over-fondness for expensive French wine. He dressed more flamboyantly than many townspeople thought was appropriate in one who made his living by turning whales into a bad smell on the east wind, into what the magistrates had called 'nuisances'. But his flamboyance was flawed; his mustard-coloured waistcoat was stained with wine, his wine-coloured waistcoat was stained with mustard. He had a habit of bursting into his office, removing his brimmed hat with a flourish and in the same movement tossing it towards the hat stand in the corner, but he lacked the hand–eye co-ordination to make an accomplishment of the gesture, and the sophistication to pick the hat up from the floor, which is where it remained until he needed it again. His leather boots had higher heels than he could walk in comfortably. They compensated for the stature that nature had denied him, but they made him walk precariously, an uncertain gait which he tried to hide by swaggering use of his forearms and thrusting stomach and which was much mimicked by giggling single files of street urchins.

His taste for theatrical gestures had led him into a mild flirtation with the old Seagate Theatre and out-rageous flirtation with selected members of the cast. He put money into it and considered buying it, eager to raise his profile from the city's C-list celebrity to its A-list, but he made his serious money from dead whales, which was always going to be a drawback to his social ambition, and behind his back Dundee was more apt to call him Greasy Johnny than Mr Woods.

And whereas the jute barons built their mansions on the furthest, most fragrant fringes of the city with views over field and estuary, John Woods built Woods Cot-tage in East Dock Street within sight and sound and smell of his factory. Whale oil, you might say, was in his blood. His industry's relationship with the jute industry was like the meadow pipit's to the infant cuckoo. It dwarfed him, it stood there with its huge mouth agape demanding to be fed, and he spent his working hours trying to satisfy the needs of that which could never be satisfied, and the retch-inducing stench of it all was in his nostrils night and day.

So when the Tay Whale turned up and the crowds flocked to the shore and roared their approval of its spectacular and occasionally haunting presence, John

Woods watched the whale and then he watched the crowd, and what he saw was theatre, wild and unpredictable and unscripted and utterly compelling (for it drew the crowds back day after day for six weeks), and John Woods loved theatre. He loved a performance, and in that regard the whale was a star attraction. He loved full houses too, and the whale guaranteed those. He also reasoned that in hard commercial terms, the whale – like all whales – was worthless while it lived. But if it could be killed, and if after death it could by some theatrical sleight of hand still be made to resemble the whale when it lived, he could give the people a show they would never forget, and he might make himself as famous as the Tay Whale itself.

So he became a theatre director. He had an unwritten script in his head, a star who had no intention of signing the unwritten contract he had in mind, his stage was the Dundee waterfront, his audience was the agog citizenry, and he began to plan for a national tour; even the great cities of Europe and America were not out of reach when Greasy Johnny started to daydream. And remarkably, he made most of it happen, and when the great museums of Europe and America came courting him, he turned them down, and selflessly donated to the local museum that which his home city had come to think of as its own.

He let it be known, as surreptitiously as possible (for even in the fetid world of whale-boilers there were envies and rivalries and old scores unsettled) that there would be a memorable payday for the whaler crew that landed the Tay Whale at Dundee docks. It may be that word of his involvement galvanised the whalers out of their sluggish early involvement in the whale hunt; it probably did not occur to them that they were already cast as bit-part players in his grand pageant. And when the pageant degenerated into grotesque pantomime, the only person who was happy with the squalid turn of events was John Wood. It is true that it took so much longer to land his star attraction that it cost him a great deal more than he had planned. But at every inglorious step of the way, the Tay Whale made more and more headlines, and these travelled the length and breadth of Britain, and no carefully constructed public relations exercise on behalf of his theatrical production could have paved the way to greater effect.

Woods was a face in the crowd at every step of the way, and he enjoyed himself hugely. For there was to be one other co-star in his production, one human face that would grab its share of the limelight alongside the Tay Whale, and that was John Woods himself.

When the whale escaped with three harpoons in it and the whalers slunk back to Dundee with nothing to show for a night at sea, he sought out two old whaling skippers with whom he had shared the occasional bottle of claret, and each told him independently that the fishermen from Broughty Ferry would find it in a day or two, and it would be dead on the surface, or beached on a quiet ebb along the Angus shore. They would let him know. He thanked them, but he made it his business to ensure that he knew before they did, and he went among the fishermen at 'The Ferry' (as Dundee styles its old fishing port) and with a bottle here and coin or two there he bought new sources of intelligence. He was thinking on his feet, ready for anything, and as the Dundee whalers had got more or less everything wrong up to that point, he was also prepared to anticipate that they could be wrong about the next bit too. So it proved. He let the unscripted twists in the plot do his work for him, sending a trusted representative up the coast when, after that nerve-jangling week in which the whale went about the business of dying with what little dignity was still available, it resurfaced much further north than the old whaling skippers had predicted, and the next scenes in his pageant shifted to Gourdon, then to Stonehaven.

So it was at Stonehaven that the landlubber component of the east coast of Scotland first made the acquaintance of the Tay Whale at close quarters. As the tide withdrew and the whole mass of the animal lay on the shore, water suddenly began to pour from it, and over minutes it deflated to something like its natural living girth, although there was nothing less natural on earth than the spectacle on offer. Stonehaven was never a whaler's port, and there could never be the same relationship with the creature that Dundee had already established, and would consummate over the next 125 years. The crowd of townspeople that had gathered in the half-dark of that early January early morning must have looked down at its prostrate carcase with something between bewilderment and profound distaste. They were accustomed to the omnipresent smell of freshly caught fish, and it sustained the economy of the town. But why would anyone make a fuss out of this putrid, shapeless slab? Not that it stopped them coming to stand and stare and point and scoff, and a few wept over that most forlorn and publicly exhibited of corpses, its belly ripped open by seabirds, its upper body bristling with the Dundee whalers' missiles.

The fishermen who had landed it lost no time in striking a deal with some canny fish merchant who knew gold dust when he saw it. There was doubtless a murmur of disbelief that went through the crowd at the news that the fishermen had been paid £10 a head for their labours, about £600 at today's prices. So the merchant paid out around £150, and there were a few on that shore who thought him quite mad, madder still when work began cleaning up the corpse in preparation for an auction the following day. It was generally made as presentable as any dead whale can be, although no attempt was made to remove the harpoon or the various spikes and bolts, the souvenirs of battle. The merchant knew his market better than the mob, and when word of the auction was sent back to John Woods in Dundee by his travelling representative he sent explicit instructions by return. His preparations were far advanced. A tug boat was standing by. Whatever it took, he must have the Tay Whale.

If anything, the crowd was bigger. Business was surprisingly brisk. But it became clear that there were only two serious bidders – John Woods and Professor Charles Struthers of Aberdeen University; Greasy Johnny the oil merchant with a taste for populist theatre and another taste for making money, and the biology professor whose ambitions were wholly scientific. It also lent the proceedings a competitive frisson between that coast's two great commercial rivals, Dundee and Aberdeen, and, in the minds of some observers at least, the respective ambitions of the rival camps in the matter of the whale's future encapsulated the distinct characters of the two cities. You might also conclude that the auction and the motives of the bidders were the most grotesque indignities that had yet been heaped on a creature that sang its way round the oceans of the world.

The bidding stopped at £226, about £12,000 in today's money. The whale was Greasy Johnny's. The professor was aghast at the thought. But he reckoned without the most surprising trait in Greasy Johnny's complex character; his appetite for grand gestures also embraced his generosity. The professor was invited to make measurements of the whale on the beach at Stonehaven, and to accompany it to Dundee, where he would be able to make a thorough examination of it at Greasy Johnny's yard. He probably failed to realise that by accepting the invitation he was instantly recruited to the growing cast of the Tay Whale Show. Greasy Johnny wasn't about to pass up the chance to feature a walk-on part for a toff in a top hat.

The tug *Excelsior* arrived from Dundee the morning after the auction. If Greasy Johnny missed the irony of using a Dundee tug to tow the whale that had so recently towed a Dundee tug in the opposite direction, it was tellingly underlined for him in a newspaper report. Alas, it is not clear which newspaper, but judging by the reporter's vicious vitriolic PS, it was surely one based furth of Dundee. The heading is simply: 'THE DUNDEE WHALE', then there is this:

A good deal has been heard lately concerning 'the Dundee whale'. Dundee has long been famous for whale fishing, but it is news to hear that it breeds them. The term 'Dundee whale', however, may simply mean that this one paid Dundee a voluntary visit. That it should have selected Dundee was not inappropriate. Perhaps it had in view something of the nature of a reprisal. Dundee has made war against whales for a long period, and it was possibly a satisfaction to this one, on that account, to be able to run away with a Dundee steam tug. But as usual, Dundee has had the best of it. The dead whale has been caught, and sold – it is not explained by whom – to a Dundee merchant. Seeing that while it lived it towed the tugs, the tugs are going to tow it now that it is dead. It is going to be lifted by hydraulic power from the sea, sixty horses have been selected for the landward portion of its last journey. Dundee is great. It yields large homage to its victims, even after they are gone, and this whale has undoubtedly by its somewhat eccentric action secured for itself an immortality. Even a Dundee wife-beater does his work with a refinement which is equalled nowhere else, and the man who adulterates milk in that town is obviously fit to be president of the British Association. But the whale has really had a good time. If as much fuss were to be made about every human being finding it possible to visit Dundee, life would be worth living, and there would be some recompense for the 'bitter end' if one could be sure of being raised by hydraulic power and drawn along in state by sixty horses.

It is fair to say that newspaper coverage of the whole Tay Whale saga was liberally laced with sarcasm, but that report has a sinister edge that still chills.

The *Excelsior* attached a hefty hawser to the tail of the whale, and a second line just in case. No one was being allowed to forget the farcical elements of the whale's escape even though the whale was now dead and the sea docile. 'Shortly after midday, the tug steamed out the harbour with its strange freight, which, at a distance, had a most remarkable likeness to a boat turned bottom up,' reported the *Advertiser*. 'The side flippers offered considerable resistance to the water, and caused the carcase to rock and sway from side to side in its progress, the flippers occasionally coming above the water . . . A pretty large number of strangers paid a visit to the monster previous to its removal, and as it left the harbour ringing cheers were raised by a great crowd of interested onlookers.'

Progress was slow. The whale, even when it was mortally wounded, made lighter work of towing the *Iron King* and its little flotilla of whaling hangers-on than the *Excelsior* made of towing the deadweight whale. It took 12 hours to cover 40 miles, so it was midnight before the *Excelsior* nosed into Victoria Dock. Bear in mind that it was midwinter, the 11th of January, and that it had been dark and frosty for around six hours, yet such is the pulling power of whales, and such was the head of steam that had built up around the story of this whale in particular, that a crowd of people at least 2,000-strong was there to greet the return of what the citizens of Dundee now considered their prodigal son. It hardly seemed to matter that the whale was dead, nor that it had died in circumstances that cast a less than flattering light on the city: it was home, and Dundee, ever the most hospitable of cities, was there to welcome it.

Meanwhile, John Woods had been busy. He had secured the services of the Victoria Dock's 70-ton hydraulic crane. He had assembled a posse of carters, each with a horse or two (about twenty in all, not the sixty that the anonymous journalist with a chip on his shoulder had predicted), and half a dozen sturdy lorries, two of which had been lashed together, ready to receive the whale. Half a mile away, his factory yard was ready to accommodate the final return of the prodigal, and the hordes who (Greasy Johnny loudly assured everyone within earshot) would flock to see the monster.

What made the bizarre occasion all the more unforgettable was that a full moon shone from a clear sky. It was as if the theatre director had specified it to lend eerie majesty to his finest hour. In the history of Scottish theatre, no grand drama was ever more powerfully lit.

The audience suddenly began to stir out of its prolonged lethargy. The received wisdom, of which there was inevitably a great deal in such a crowd, had been that the whale would now have to lie in the water until daylight, and the crowd was restlessly resigned to shuffling its disappointment off into the night. But the moment it became clear that the great crane was about to become the centre stage of the next act, there was a frenzied mass sprint along the quayside for the best vantage points. The mood of the crowd transformed. 'Some lively chaff was indulged in by the spectators, and much amusement was created by a man getting on the whale's back and executing a series of acrobatic feats', the *Advertiser* reported. It is not clear whether the whale was in or out of the water at this point, but it must surely be the first time in the history of whaling that a whale corpse was used as a trampoline.

Coils of chain were wound round the tail of the whale, and the crane's massive hook took hold, and a new intensity gripped the crowd: would the slender rump of the whale stand the strain, or would the infinitely heavier front portion snap off and fall into the dock, thereby rendering worthless the entire operation from first harpoon to the *Excelsior*'s meticulously negotiated arrival through the dock gate, and scuppering Greasy John's ambitions at a stroke? Wagers were struck, for and against the successful raising of the whale in one piece. The huge tail drew gasps from 1,000 throats as it was lifted clear of the water, the first time the crowd had seen it at such close quarters, though many on the quayside that night were veteran observers of the whale's carefree antics in the estuary weeks before. Inch by inch, the whale transformed from something that looked like an overturned hull into something the world might never have seen before, a whale suspended head down and vertically over dry land by the light of a full moon. Someone in the crowd yelled: 'Three cheers for the Tay Whale' and 2,000 opened throats responded.

Greasy Johnny had had this moment in mind for

some time, even if the presence of the full moon was a spectacular fluke. Dundee photographer Charles Johnson was recruited to immortalise it and, bearing in mind that newspaper photography at the time was more or less non-existent, and both the equipment and the evolution of the photographic art were still in their infancy, the result is remarkable. (Less remarkable, and less worthy of the art, was the decision to superimpose the whale lying in the unphotogenic surroundings of Greasy Johnny's yard on a second photograph of a sunset over the Tay. Still, he was not the last photographer to manipulate reality to pander to popular appeal. Greasy Johnny, I would imagine, approved heartily.)

While the suspended whale was being manoeuvred into position above the waiting lorries, and while those who had wagered against a successful outcome began reluctantly to stump up, it was suddenly noticed that the whale appeared to be growing longer by the moment.

Was it stretching under its own weight?

Was that what happened when you suspended such a monster by the tail?

Perhaps the thing might break apart yet?

Then it became clear what was happening. The whale's tongue was falling out of its mouth. One moment it was slithering out into the moonlight, the next, it became too heavy for its own anchorage deep in the throat of the whale, and fell out into the dock, where it sank. It was not quite how the doom-mongers had envisaged the whale breaking apart, but it added unique spice to those who waged the wager argument.

So the tongueless whale was edged down to where the two lashed lorries awaited it. The crane set it down as gently as a baby on a mother's knee. The springs on the lorries creaked and groaned and shattered, and the crane lifted the whale aloft again. The crowd roared. This was worth the long wait in the January night. Greasy Johnny grinned to himself, despite the fact that these were his lorries that had been wrecked. He had half expected it. He commanded them to be hauled away, and two much heftier vehicles were wheeled into place, and again they were lashed together, and again the whale was lowered into place, and again the springs protested, but this time they held. The horses meekly took up their positions. They were long accustomed to hefting strange burdens at their masters' bidding, and this one was no different, except that it smelled worse than most. But in any case, 20 straining workhorses produce their own distinctive aroma. The wheels rumbled, the whale moved, the crowd cheered again, then groaned as the wheels splayed out from their useless axles after a few yards.

Greasy Johnny called in the big guns. It is tempting to imagine that he had orchestrated even this, just to hold the crowds, to delight the journalists, to raise the standing of his prize whale in the eyes of the watching world. He summoned a huge bogie whose day job was transporting industrial boilers, and commanded it to moonlight a dead whale. He ushered in more horses. (I imagine these held discreetly in a nearby warehouse, not to be led out until a pre-arranged signal announced the arrival of the bogie). There were now 30 horses in all, and these reinforcements were hitched without fuss to the front of the queue. And bathed by the huge, low, full moon that now laid a broad furrow of brilliant silver light across the mile-wide Tay estuary, the mightily reinforced procession rumbled forward. The clatter of horseshoes, the shouts of the carters, the groan of iron wheels on stone streets, and the excited banter and shuffling footfalls of most of the assembled crowd were welded into a cacophony of such unscriptable weirdness that Greasy Johnny, stuff-strutting like a pipe major at the head of the leading horse, laughed aloud at the wonder of his own genius. Not even Shakespeare, he told himself, would have dreamed of such daring.

And superimposed upon it all, beyond pain, beyond fear, beyond life, the Tay Whale stared sightlessly forward.

'The fish was much improved in appearance after being taken out of the water,' wrote the *Advertiser*'s man:

The fins and tail were white, and the glossy skin appeared beautiful in the moonlight. The whale will be exhibited in

Mr Woods' premises in East Dock Street for a few days. The operations were carried out with skill and coolness, and those who witnessed the strange scene will not soon forget it.

It is stated that several scientific gentlemen from different parts of the country are anxious to secure the skeleton of this rare visitor to our latitudes, and that it is therefore doubtful where its bones may ultimately find their last resting-place.

Uh-huh, I detect the hand of Greasy Johnny again, playing off one 'scientific gentleman' against another, ratcheting up the price, either as an insurance policy against the commercial failure of his immediate plans (unlikely, his actions thus far were not those of a man who spends much time contemplating failure), or, more likely, enhancing the magnitude of the decision he had already made to donate the skeleton to his home city. This was, after all, the *Tay* Whale, and he had, after all, brought it 'home'. For the next 125 years, it would occur to no one that its home could possibly be anywhere else.

Yet this was an animal that could have travelled the oceans of the world for 200 years, singing.

Chapter 9

Life After Death

Then hurrah! for the mighty monster whale,
Which has got 17 feet 4 inches from tip to tip of a tail!
Which can be seen for a sixpence or a shilling,
That is to say, if the people are willing . . .
                                        William McGonagall
                                        'The Famous Tay Whale'

'Have you seen the whale?' was the interrogation that
met one on every hand in Dundee and its neighbourhood yesterday. To give a negative reply to the query
was to put oneself in the position of a person justly
entitled to universal and unbounded pity; and it may
be surmised that there were few who had the courage
to deny a visual acquaintance with the monster that
has added so much to the fame of the 'silvery Tay'. As
a matter of fact, however, almost everybody has seen
the whale . . . The Dundonians are, naturally, proud
of their whale, but it may be questioned whether a
good many of them would not have preferred that his
whaleship had been allowed to enjoy his large life in
his native deeps, instead of being laid on his back in an
oil yard . . . It would, of course, have been too much
to expect that he would have taken up his quarters
permanently in the Tay; but he might have taken

kindly to the beautiful estuary, and paid it periodic visits – and surely this would have been honour enough to Dundee. But this is mere idle sentiment. Whales exist only to be captured and converted into oil and other things of commercial value. Therefore, when one appeared in the Tay last month the desire to get hold of him, for the purpose of converting into as much money as possible, was one of the most natural that could be entertained.

The *Advertiser*
January 1884

The Procession travelled the half-mile to John Woods's yard without further mishap, but Further Mishap had simply travelled faster than the laborious progress of the whale and was lurking just inside the yard. Greasy Johnny's preparations had been so swift and the results so spectacular that some overlooked shortcoming was more or less inevitable. It kicked in on his doorstep. The huge weight of the bogie, with the addition of the 26-ton whale, encountered the soft earth of the yard and declined to go any further. Its wheels bedded down and stuck fast. The only solution was to jack up the bogie, a slow, filthy, malodorous, labour-intensive slog of an operation. The result was that the whale reached its destination (though far from its final resting place) more or less 24 hours after it had begun its weird landward journey half a mile away at Victoria Dock.

And Further Mishap had one more little trick up its mischievous sleeve. A nicely turned paragraph in the anonymous 1884 pamphlet, *The History of the Whale*, explains:

> At the conclusion of the operation an incident occurred which, without reaching the dignity of the previous accidents, narrowly missed outshining them all. A number of naphtha lamps had been used for shedding light on the work of getting the fish in at the gateway, and at the close these were stored in one of the outhouses on the premises. Some of the oil had been spilled and caught fire, which rapidly spread. Mr Woods and some assistants promptly threw a number of saturated cloths over the flames, and fortunately succeeded in quelling the fire, or the fish, which had already been shot, drowned, and hanged at the crane, might have missed its destiny of boiling, by being prematurely roasted.

Considering all that had gone before and all that was about to befall the Tay Whale, a swift roasting might have been kinder. Meanwhile divers recruited by Greasy Johnny carried out one of their more unlikely operations: they recovered the whale's tongue from the Victoria Dock. God knows why, or what was done with it once it was brought to Woods's premises, and once it was weighed. (It weighed half a ton.) What can you do with the tongue of a whale that has been dead for more than a week, a tongue whose condition was surely not improved by spending a night at the bottom of the Victoria Dock? But that was the least of the indignities that lay in wait. At least the tongue fell out of its own accord. The rest of the whale had to be forcibly excavated before Greasy Johnny's masterplan could be implemented.

By the following Saturday, he was ready to start receiving paying guests at his yard. He had already paid out over £400 to bring the whale home, including what some saw as a niggardly half-sovereign a man to the Dundee crews who harpooned it. He was now ready to recoup his investment. He opened his gates to the world, and invited them to come in and see the whale – for a small fee: between 9 a.m and 4 p.m. the fee was one shilling; between 4 p.m and 9 p.m it was sixpence. He had anticipated brisk business. He alerted the railway companies who laid on special excursions from Perth, sundry Angus towns and from Fife. That first day, 12,000 people came. Many more were turned away. Say for the sake of argument that 8,000 paid a shilling and 4,000 paid sixpence, which is a reasonable enough estimate. At 20 shillings in the pound, that's £500 on the first day. Greasy Johnny had struck pay-dirt.

Early the following week, local newspapers carried an advertisement that began: 'THE TAY WHALE. Now on exhibition at Mr Woods' oil establishment, End of

East Dock Street, until further notice. Mr Woods takes this opportunity of apologising to the Thousands of People disappointed on Saturday, but . . .' and the gist of the 'but' was that they should try again. They did, and in two weeks, 50,000 people had paid for the privilege of eyeballing the Tay Whale at close quarters.

And then, just when I had become convinced that Woods was an opportunist money-grabbing son-of-a-bitch, I stumbled on this among the old press reports: 'Mr Woods has kindly arranged for the free exhibition of the whale to the boys of the Morgan Hospital, the boys and girls in the Royal Orphan Institution, the Deaf and Dumb Institution, the boys of the Industrial School, Baldovan, the girls of the Industrial School, Ward Road, and the inmates of East and West Poorhouses.'

One hundred and twenty-five years after the event, Greasy Johnny is not an easy figure to pin down, and I suspect it was no easier at the time. Besides, Greasy Johnny was not the only one to cash in on the phenomenon of the Tay Whale. Local photographers periodically set up a table and chair *inside* its propped-open mouth, and for three shillings you could sit there for a portrait. Why you would want to is another matter, but there were many takers, the fashionable formality of the poses rather at odds with the surroundings and the niggling suspicion among viewers of the subsequent portraits that here were people trying very hard to hold their breath just a little longer.

I was horrified when I first read about this. Perhaps it was a joke? I hoped against hope that even in the economic and social climate of the 1880s, when the only good whale was a dead whale, even in Dundee that made such a good living out of dead whales, the natives' sense of just the most basic, common decency would have stopped well short of posing for a photograph inside its mouth, and that somehow adding the table and chair was surely a kind of *Addams Family* twist to the joke in execrable taste. But it was no joke. It happened, and as with everything to do with the Tay Whale's commercial life after death, business was brisk.

And if you thought the idea of a human being wandering into the open mouth of a whale only happened in the Bible and was about as credible as fitting two of every species on earth into an ark, be assured there was room to spare in that mouth not just for a table and chair but also for a three-piece suite and an upright piano. Here, for example, is a more reliable witness than Jonah, Roger Payne writing in *Among Whales*:

When you and I say the whale opens its mouth 'wide' we may have a kind of mental picture about the process . . . But I can assure you that no-one is ever properly prepared for the degree to which a humpback whale can open its mouth. I have witnessed a humpback repeatedly open its mouth more than ninety degrees. And I have, by making an off-the-cuff calculation, satisfied myself that it could have comfortably engulfed a medium-sized car in the cavern of its gape. I have a friend who was studying humpbacks in Alaska when one of them rose beneath his boat. The next thing he knew he and the boat were inside its widely opened mouth, a situation that only lasted for a second as the whale was apparently as surprised as he and instantly backed off. But he observed that when his Zodiac was in the whale's mouth it was not grounded on the whale's jaws but was floating freely, with water under its keel.

The man from the *Advertiser*, who clearly revelled in his reporting duties throughout the saga of the whale, and took more than his share of liberties, was there when the gates of Greasy Johnny's yard were finally closed to the public. He offered this retrospective:

Although he has not been looking quite his best since he was brought to *terra firma,* his appearance has certainly made a great impression on the public mind. Thousands of people have flocked to his *matinees* and his evening parties on the invitation of Mr Wood, his enterprising purchaser. Every day, however, he became less attractive to the eyes and especially to the noses of his visitors. It has been a source of disappointment to a great many people not previously acquainted with whales that his only recognisable feature was his tail. This slight defect in his appearance, it may be mentioned, is now intended to be remedied, for we understand that, after the work of removing the too-rapidly decomposing portions of his structure has been completed, these are to be replaced by a wooden framework, which will give what is left of him, as nearly as possible, his proper outline.

The worst appearance, without exception, that ever the gigantic cetacean made was yesterday . . .

Ah yes, the dissecting and embalming had just begun.

Professor John Struthers of Aberdeen University, who came second to Greasy Johnny at the Stonehaven auction, had nevertheless continued to follow every twist and turn of the whale's afterlife. He and Greasy Johnny had both realised at more or less the same time that each could be of use to the other in pursuit of their very different ambitions for the whale, and struck up an unlikely relationship. It survived Greasy Johnny's change of mind about the final destination of the skeleton. He had originally agreed to the professor's request to give it to Aberdeen in exchange for services rendered, but such was the level of interest in the creature in Dundee, he had sat down a few days before the professor's arrival and written the following letter:

East Dock Street,
Dundee
21st January, 1884

To the Provost and Magistrates of the Royal Burgh of
Dundee

The Tay Whale

Gentlemen,

I have much pleasure in intimating to you that when
done exhibiting the above monster, and when dissected
by the learned professors, I will be happy to hand over
the remains to you for presentation to the town of
Dundee, so that the skeleton may be secured for our
own museum.

Yours very truly,

JOHN WOODS

The letter was warmly received at a special meeting of
the council, where it was agreed that Mr Woods should
be thanked for his patriotic gesture in the face of strong
interest from many other museums which had been
'anxious to secure the fish'.

The relationship between Greasy Johnny and the
professor even survived the professor's discovery, when
he arrived in Dundee to perform the partial dissection
and embalmment of the whale, that he had been cast as
a kind of head clown in a setting that owed more to a

circus than a scientific laboratory. Greasy Johnny, of course, was the ringmaster.

Again, you can't help but be impressed both by the speed and general efficiency with which he made things happen, all of it with a certain dramatic flair that veered between the outrageous and the hideous. So the professor, aided by Mr Robert Gibb of the Aberdeen Anatomical Museum and Mr George Sim who is simply described as 'a naturalist', arrived at the Woods yard to find an area enclosed by small grandstands, and in its centre a large wooden platform on which the whale lay, belly-up as he had requested. The grandstands were for invited guests, including medical experts from the city and its surrounding area, clergymen (Why clergymen? Did they expect the first incision to unearth a Jonah-like revelation?), whaling captains (as if they hadn't seen enough dead whales in their time) and sundry civic dignitaries. The guests may have been invited, but they were expected to pay sweetly for the privilege of being invited – half a crown. Greasy Johnny probably reasoned that (a) they wouldn't want not to be on the list and (b) they could all afford it. The whole area had been floored with sawdust, and as if that didn't serve the illusion of a circus well enough, Greasy Johnny had hired a band. Much to the irritation of the professor, the band of the Forfarshire Rifle Volunteers played 'appropriate music'. It was a tough gig for the band. One of many press reports noted: 'Shortly before eleven the band of the 1st F.R.V. marched into the enclosure . . . It may be presumed that the conductor had found it impossible to arrange a programme consisting of music appropriate to the dissection of a whale, for the airs discoursed during the day were of a popular and lively character.'

Something like 'Whale Meat Again' perhaps? ('Whale meat again, don't know where, don't know when, but there'll be whale meet again some sunny day . . .')

But the gathering was there to witness the surgical humiliation of the whale and, just as likely, to be seen to be there, for by now the whale was an object of endless fascination for the nation's press as well as the only subject in town worth talking about. Professor Struthers made the first incision near the tail and carried it forward to near the mouth. The skin, with its four-inch-thick layer of blubber, was drawn back using a block and tackle, which sounds more industrial than surgical, but then the incision was made with a flensing knife, not a scalpel, and in Dundee in 1884, there were few things more symbolic of heavy industry than a dead whale. The stomach was thus exposed. 'The viscera, together with pelvic bones and rudimentary hind limbs and surrounding flesh were placed in casks . . . the vast quantity of matter in the inside of the whale created great surprise among uninitiated observers.' God knows why. But three hours fairly flew by while the flesh and blubber were cut away from the skeleton and carefully stowed in barrels to be boiled for oil. This was, it should be remembered, still an oil merchant's yard and not a university campus and not a circus, and for all the oil merchant's dramatic flair and entrepreneurial skills, he was still an oil merchant. Meanwhile, the viscera were finally exposed, and the band played on while the disembowelment proceeded.

The tail muscle was exposed. It was 'nearly the girth of a man's body'. But it seems that everyone wanted to see the heart. It proved to be 'a ponderous mass of flesh and quite filled a large barrel'. We know this because a squad of whalers had also been recruited to delve into the whale's innards and remove those organs, bones and other items of scientific interest that the professor identified. Irony doesn't get much grimmer than this. Some of the very men whom the whale had defeated in the last hours of its life, and who were consoled by Greasy Johnny with a half-sovereign apiece, now added to their income from the whale they had failed to deliver by wresting the very heart from its body. It is fair to say that more than the irony was grim. The frightful nature of that particular labour would have to be seen to be believed, and for that matter, it would have to be smelled to be believed too. Among the eye-witness reports was this: 'The proceedings at first were watched with a good deal of interest by the spectators . . . but as the work progressed, the stench emanating from the

113

carcase proved too strong for a good many. Those who had first crowded round the operators gradually retreated to a safe distance and held their noses . . .'

So sundry barrels of whale components – including much of the skeleton – were readied for transport to Aberdeen University, and over the next two days the innards of the whale were embalmed with vast quantities of carbolic acid. Then a wooden frame was pushed into the skin, effectively replacing the skeleton, and yet more vast quantities, this time of straw, were stuffed into the skin until it once more began to bear a passing resemblance to a humpback whale. It was in this guise – devoid of blubber, flesh, heart, lungs, stomach, intestines, bone and muscle, to name but a few shortcomings – that the Tay Whale was readied to go on a tour of Britain, a journey by a humpback whale that never touched water. It is hard to imagine a more outrageous fraud, or for that matter a more comprehensively insulted and exploited animal. And this, remember, was a whale that might have travelled the oceans of the world for 200 years.

Something of the unsavoury flavour of all this was caught in a report in the *Scotsman* which more than hinted at the circus element of Greasy Johnny's approach, as it appeared to coincide with a certain London circus owner's attempts to palm off a piebald elephant as genuine:

It was naturally expected that this would be the 'beginning of the end' so far as the career of that unfortunate whale was concerned. After affording exciting sport to the whalers in the Tay, giving startling exhibitions of the giant strength with which he was endowed, dying a lingering death in the solitude of an unknown sea, being lost and found, bought and sold, exhibited to gazing thousands, and making a 'pile' of goodly proportions for an enterprising purchaser – the whale might surely have been allowed to complete his mission by submitting his several parts to the process which the Dundee oil merchants had decreed for whales. But it has been decided to keep up the excitement in the public mind for some time longer, and after the straw or other substance has been substituted for the internal fittings, and the body has been submitted to some kind of embalming process, his whaleship will go on tour.

He is first to 'star' in the provinces, and will ultimately find his way to London, about the period when perhaps the Cockneys have completely settled in their minds that the piebald elephant is a zoological humbug, and that Barnum has been to some extent 'bamboozling' them. As a piece of enterprise, this tour seems to reflect credit and courage and pluck upon the party who has turned the excitement over the whale to such profitable account. It indicates a canny appreciation of the importance of striking while the iron is hot. The scheme has been gratuitously advertised. Barnum could not have wished better luck in this respect if the whale had been his, and he had sent it on tour. In fact, the great showman will be jealous lest his precious pachyderm should shine with greatly diminished splendour when he comes into competition with the whale of the Tay.

But from another point of view – the sanitary aspect of the subject – it is doubtful whether the interests of the public are consulted by allowing this putrefying mass of oil and blubber to be paraded through the country. Those who saw it in Dundee many days ago are under the impression that they smell it still. The question may, therefore, suggest itself to local authorities whether this whale is not being carried a little too far.

Ah, if only, but by the time that particular scribe put pen to paper, there was an unstoppable head of steam fuelling the whale's progress, and the smile on Greasy Johnny's face was wide enough to accommodate a table and chair and a photographer's model, and the boost to his bank balance would have quite filled a large barrel.

But Greasy Johnny, Professor Struthers and sundry photographers were not the only ones intent on advancing their careers on the back of the Tay Whale. There was another face in the stands at Greasy Johnny's yard who took advantage of a lull in the repertoire of the band of the 1st Forfar Rifles Volunteers to peddle his wares. He was 'a long-haired gentleman in a black surtout and slouched hat calling the attention of the spectators to a poem, *apropos* of the whale, of which he proclaimed himself the author . . .'

Chapter 10

The McGonagall Effect

The most startling incident in my life was the time I discovered myself to be a poet, which was in the year 1877. During the Dundee holiday week, in the bright and balmy month of June, when trees and flowers were in full bloom, while lonely and sad in my room, I sat thinking about the thousands of people who were away by rail and steamboat, perhaps to the land of Burns, or poor ill-treated Tannahill, or to gaze upon the Trossachs in Rob Roy's country, or elsewhere wherever their minds led them. While pondering so, I seemed to feel, as it were, a strange kind of feeling stealing over me, and I remained so for about five minutes. A flame, as Lord Byron has said, seemed to kindle up my entire frame along with a strong desire to write poetry; and I felt so happy, so happy, that I was inclined to dance, then I began to pace backwards and forwards in the room, trying to shake off all thought of writing poetry; but the more I tried, the more strong the sensation became. It was so strong I imagined that a pen was in my right hand, and a voice crying, 'Write! Write!'

William McGonagall
A Brief Autobiography, 1890

In the five and a half years between the most startling incident in William McGonagall's life and the Famous Tay Whale's arrival on his doorstep, he had become famous, a figure of fun and occasionally ridicule and the butt of academic jokes to be sure, but he had also travelled far on his way to becoming the most popular poet after Burns that Scotland had ever known. When his *Poetic Gems* was first published as two volumes in 1890 by Dundee publishers David Winter (who had also printed the original broadsheets for McGonagall himself), it was the beginning of a publishing phenomenon. It was followed in due course by *More Poetic Gems*. My crumbling 1966 paperback edition of *Poetic Gems*, also published by Winter, was the fourteenth impression and I shudder to think of the royalties it must have heaped up since then. In 2007, a new *Collected Poems* was published. The fame of John Woods more or less died with him in 1895; McGonagall died in 1902 and more than 100 years later the elusive appeal of his poetry is undiminished, and his star has never burned brighter.

Billy Connolly famously read him on TV and in a ferocious blizzard while standing on the top of the Law, Dundee's old volcanic centrepiece. Spike Milligan made a more or less hysterical programme about him. Scots academics have raged against him for over a century. But the most ferocious assault on him was by Kurt Wittig, a German critic whose 1958 book, *The Scottish*

The Winter Whale

Tradition in Literature, is something of a bible among students of Scottish literary criticism:

> The *Poetic Gems* of The Great William McGonagall, poet and tragedian [which is how McGonagall fondly styled himself], and shabbiest of public house rhymesters, are still reprinted almost every year; and their continuing popularity would indeed be an interesting problem for a psychiatrist to study. It is not rock-bottom that we touch here, that would suggest something solid; with him, poetry is irretrievably sunk in mire.

Professor Douglas Gifford of Glasgow University was infinitely more tolerant and thoughtful in his *The History of Scottish Literature*:

> It is usually assumed that McGonagall is enjoyed because he is unintentionally amusing and everyone likes a good laugh. True, if dubiously defensible. But we know from tested public performance, that an actor with a good voice can read the best of McGonagall (e.g. 'The Little Match Girl') quite straight and with some pathos . . . If voice seems to be the key, we perhaps direct ourselves to Hamish Henderson's argument that the clumsy ametricality of the lines (on the page) can be related to McGonagall's Irish family background of 'come-all-ye' folk song, the value of his poems being no more than that of their originality in uniquely and consistently forming

their style out of the detritus of folk poetry. Perhaps anything carried to an extreme is attractive, as Blake claimed . . . The obvious 'badness' of McGonagall also does not cancel the genuine popular appeal of someone who, unlike many of his contemporaries, gave himself the function of commenting on the noted public events of the time.

And what events! The first railway bridge across the Tay, the Tay Bridge disaster and the new railway bridge across the Tay were all commemorated by McGonagall. All three had the same first line – 'Beautiful Railway Bridge of the Silvery Tay!', except that in the third poem the word 'new' was inserted between 'Beautiful' and 'Railway', and his relaxed attitude to metre allowed him to get away with it. That relaxed attitude allied to a sly sense of humour allowed him to slip his funniest couplet into 'An Ode to the Queen on Her Jubilee Year':

> Oh! try and make her happy in country and town,
> And not with Shakespeare say, 'uneasy lies the
>   head that wears a crown'.

Shakespeare was McGonagall's inspiration. He learned huge chunks of *Macbeth* and *Hamlet* and *Richard III* when he was little more than a child, and performed them as a young man whenever and wherever he could find or improvise a stage. He was a hand-loom weaver by trade but he was an actor at heart, and that passion determined the kind of poet he became. Mostly, he did not write poetry, but rather scripts to perform. He was, as Professor Gifford pointed out, a performance poet, and his sense of theatre was as important to his work as the words on the page. The recurring, predictable rhyming words and phrases that are everywhere through the poems were what his audiences expected, and where they joined in, much like a chorus in a folk song.

Whenever he performed in the pubs and the halls of Dundee, Angus, Perth and Fife, there were always raucous demands for his greatest hits – the three Tay Bridge poems, a song called 'The Rattling Boy from Dublin', his battle poems to Bannockburn, Flodden, Sheriffmuir and Culloden, anything involving Queen Victoria, for whom he had an almost obsessively patriotic affection, and inevitably, 'The Famous Tay Whale'. So it was no surprise to find him among the invited guests at Greasy Johnny's embalming shindig with copies of a new poem for sale. Theatre was in the blood of both men, and it would have both suited and flattered the ego of Greasy Johnny to spring McGonagall on his guests with a Tay Whale poem that casually name-dropped John Woods as the man who 'has brought it to Dundee all safe and all sound', and possibly McGonagall alone among the invited guests did not have to pay the half-crown admittance.

But there was also this: McGonagall alone was not named in the *Advertiser*'s account of the proceedings. He was merely referred to as that 'amusing diversion caused by a long-haired gentleman in a black surtout and slouched hat calling the attention of the spectators to a poem, *a propos* of the whale, of which he proclaimed himself the author, and which he proceeded to recite with much gusto. He afterwards announced that the poem could be obtained on payment of the sum of one penny, and condescendingly sold a few copies at that figure. There was a good deal of "Silvery Tay" in the poem . . .'

So the journalist knew well enough who he was writing about (McGonagall rarely wrote the word 'Tay' without writing the word 'silvery' first; it was one of his many signature traits), but there was something in his work and the way he conducted himself that was as offensive to some of his contemporaries as the smell of decaying whale flesh. Yet he knew his market, he wrote accessibly, and because he mostly wrote of the events and personalities of the day, and of the events of Scottish and British history, he was relevant to his audience. He took his work out into their midst and he performed it 'with much gusto'. Today he is probably more widely read than ever, there are McGonagall Suppers wherever there are Scots in the world, he has celebrity endorsements, and his royalties would keep him infinitely more comfortably today than they did in his lifetime. His poem 'An Address to the New Tay Bridge' has been carved into the pavement near the bridge, so you can walk along by the river, reading it as you go, and do try to turn a blind eye to the engraver's misspellings. It is a unique honour, nevertheless.

And it is fair to say that his is the popular voice of the Tay Whale, not just because of the many thousands of copies of *Poetic Gems* that are in the world, but it is also prominently featured alongside the skeleton in the museum's whaling display, and in tourist information panels and other publicity. Strange how such an event from the heyday of the Victorians' lust for killing wildlife and the city's old addiction to the obnoxious trade of whaling can be rendered down through the passage of time into the stuff of twenty-first-century tourism fodder, simply because the only account of it with which anyone is familiar was written by a poet whose work tends to make us smile.

No other single whale among the many thousands that died at the hands of the Dundee whalers in the eighteenth and nineteenth centuries emerges from that bloodied horde as a recognisable individual. (Between 1865 and 1883, for example, the Dundee whaling fleet alone killed over 1,400 whales.) No other account of its death kept its story alive: the rest were newspaper reports which have been more or less silent and un-consulted these last 125 years, and they vary wildly in both accuracy and detail. McGonagall alone is responsible for enshrining the events of that winter of the whale in an enduring form (not that he was particularly accurate either, but then perhaps it is not a poet's job to be accurate, but rather to take risks with language that non-poet writers would not dare to attempt, and no one can deny that McGonagall did that). I have no doubt at all that when this book is dust, McGonagall's poem will still be read often enough to keep the whale's memory alive. Even now, there is hardly a Dundee native anywhere in the world who does not think of the Tay as silvery. He put his own poetry into the language of the people and there are few enough poets who achieve that: Shakespeare and Burns, of course, but not many more.

And I concede that his poem dragged the Tay Whale from the back of my mind (where it had been stashed away since childhood) to the front. He had cropped up, inevitably, in a book I wrote a dozen years ago, *The Road and the Miles*, which had the sub-title of *A Homage to Dundee*. But even then I was receiving his take on the Tay Whale in the spirit in which it was offered. The whale was 'resolved to have some sport and play'; the whalers were 'resolved to capture the whale and have some fun' and they 'laughed and grinned just like wild baboons' (a line contrived purely to create a rhyme for 'harpoons', and just possibly, to soften the blow and dull the pain of the harpoons). His poem omits to mention that the whale died. One minute the whale is lashing the water with its tail, the next it is harpooned, it speeds off to Stonehaven, where it lies placidly on the water and the Gourdon boys slip a noose round its tail. He never says that it is a dead tail. There are no wounds, no blood, there has been no ordeal. Then hurrah for the mighty monster whale . . .

Hurrah!? He wants us to cheer!

And do you know what? We did! We cheered the boats into Stonehaven harbour. We cheered the whale when it was towed out of Stonehaven harbour. We cheered its arrival in Dundee at midnight, and again when it was raised up out of the water by the crane (the cheers turning to gasps when its tongue fell out into the water). It was cheered every step of the way as it toured the country on a railway wagon, and it was cheered when it came home again and the great charade was over. Somehow, McGonagall disarms us, renders our anger impotent. We shake our heads at the way he tells a story, but the smiles on our faces betray his place in our affections. William Topaz McGonagall gave the story of The Famous Tay Whale to the world, but the truth is that there was little enough to smile about.

Chapter 11

Northward Ho!

He was sure that when people went to look at the Tay
Whale they would say it was as ugly an object as ever
they saw – (laughter) – and that it presented no
particular feature of interest other than the hull of
a wreck on the seashore.

Newspaper report of Professor Struthers'
Aberdeen Lecture, February 1884

To anyone who has actually seen a humpback whale
up close, the concept of giving such a magnificent and
graceful creature such a pejorative name may seem
unaccountable. But these animals were named by
people who looked at them as blubber – and for
whom the grace, power, and awesome beauty of
the whale seem to have gone unnoticed.

Roger Payne
Among Whales

In the month of January, 1884, the Tay Whale had
towed a small flotilla of boats, swum free with three
harpoons in its body, died a lingering death, floated to
the surface of the North Sea, been taken in tow by 3
fishing boats, been taken in tow by a steam tug, been

hauled vertically from the sea by a 70-ton crane (a feat it used to achieve in life with a flick of its own tail), broken 4 wagons, been towed by 30 horses on an industrial bogie designed to transport boilers, been dissected, disembowelled and embalmed, had much of its skeleton replaced by wood and its flesh by straw (and in the process its weight was reduced by 11 tons), and had finally been stitched up and manhandled onto a cradle which was towed by 20 more horses from the Woods oil yard in East Dock Street, Dundee to Tay Bridge Station, a distance of about half a mile. It was now planned that on the last day of that month, and quite without any acknowledgment of irony, it should become a passenger on a train. The Tay Whale was about to go on tour.

It would be, thought Greasy Johnny, the whale's finest hour, and the mightiest of his achievements on its behalf. It was about to travel more than 60 miles over land, to Aberdeen. Surely no whale had ever made such a journey anywhere in the world. Surely no whale had been the cause of such a logistical nightmare as the one that now ensnared Greasy Johnny and his army of staff and other conscripts. This would be an unprecedented take on the old whaler's cry, 'Northward Ho!', even if it did involve travelling no further northward than Aberdeen.

And on the way, it would pass through Broughty Ferry, where the crowds had gathered around the castle a few weeks before to whoop their delight each time the whale breached, and gasped each time it blew or flourished its tail; it would pass through Arbroath where the Bell Rock Lighthouse is clearly seen a dozen miles out to sea and which the whale saw as the lowest star in the sky during its brief sojourn in the Tay estuary; it would pass through Gourdon, where the fishermen were doubtless still celebrating with the fruits of their piracy and exaggerating every detail to the very edge of credibility, the way fishermen do; it would pass through Stonehaven where they dumped the whale on its back on the shore and Greasy Johnny's representative haggled for the right to own it, and finally it would be put on show in Aberdeen where the professor who so nearly became its owner thought people would think it as ugly an object as they ever saw.

It is certainly true that a great ugliness was inflicted upon it, but it is a profoundly disappointing response from a university professor. It was as if he had not noticed that Charles Darwin had recently stood the known world on its head with his writings. In fact, the proximity of Darwin's work to the events that befell the Tay Whale cropped up in one press report, albeit in the curiously convoluted language of the day:

These notes may, it is hoped, serve in some measure to show the good folks of Dundee and the neighbourhood that they have at present an opportunity not merely of seeing a whale which is a somewhat rare one on our coasts, but of seeing a creature which is, at all times, and of whatever variety, well worth contemplating as full of instruction. The day is not long past when rudimentary structures such as those alluded to above were regarded unintelligently as mere curiosities or freaks of nature. But since the late Mr Darwin put forward his hypothesis, such structures have been looked on as having received their explanation and as furnishing strong evidence in support of the views of that illustrious observer and thinker.

You imagine the writer was thinking as he ended that less-than-crystal-clear summary of Darwin's 'hypothesis' of adding, '. . . whatever they may be' to the end of that last sentence.

It is not at all clear that Greasy Johnny had advanced far beyond the 'freaks of nature' school of thought as he and his men laboured through those last days of January to heave the whale back onto its belly (in which position its operation scar and the mutilation by seabirds were happily invisible), and manoeuvred it onto a wooden cradle in preparation for the short journey to the station. Yet it is hard not to admire his inventive industry and his ability to make things happen at speed. Less than three weeks after he had bought the whale it had been seen by 50,000 people, the extraordinary surgical operation had taken place in circus-like surroundings, and he had designed and commissioned the building of a cradle. There was no handbook to consult. The technique for arranging the transport of a dead whale by rail was a blank page, but whatever the colossal shortcomings of the Victorian era in its attitude to wildlife and wild places, there was a can-do attitude of an almost religious fervour abroad in the air and Greasy Johnny was its arch-disciple. Fifty years later, he might have been Walt Disney.

The cradle and its tarpaulin-wrapped cargo occupied the greater part of three large railway wagons, and when the train steamed off into the January night, the whale had a travelling companion too. Of all the zany ideas Greasy Johnny had embraced these last three heady weeks, the wackiest was his decision to bring in a side-show while the professor pulled the whale apart and stuck it back together again. The side show was a 'talking seal' that had been caught by a Broughty Ferry fisherman who had mysteriously decided to keep it alive (the whaling ships' other accomplishment was to kill seals by the million back then), tamed it and taught it tricks, one of which was to make noises that approximated to human words. This hapless wretch was now parcelled up and persuaded to perform on cue when and wherever the whale was unsheathed. So off they steamed into the night, the dead whale and the half-alive seal, and a vast crew of human attendants. Greasy Johnny had finally gone nuts.

'Dundee's latest wonder, that sportive scion of the

cetacean family whose frolics in the Tay were summarily brought to a close on New Year's Day, is now to go on tour,' burbled the *Advertiser*'s man, 'having ministered to the curiosity of the public of Juteopolis and neighbourhood for the last few weeks, and to the Aberdonians is to be accorded the privilege of being the first to inspect his whaleship in travelling attire. The 'monster', as the animal has been not inappropriately designated since it began its career on *terra firma,* arrived in Aberdeen last night with the North British goods train, and today, as well as on every other day this week, it will be on exhibition in a marquee at the Recreation Grounds, Inches.'

Do you think anyone at all wrote like that before Walter Scott smothered the Victorians in his word-deluges?

The train reached Aberdeen about 10 p.m. Crowds had gathered at almost every bridge and vantage point along the route, but all they had seen was a slow-moving shapelessness under a tarpaulin that wasn't quite big enough, all of it smothered in the winter darkness of the coast. However, they could all say they had seen the Tay Whale, and it seems that that was all that mattered, whether it was vigorously alive in the open sea or a corpse on a railway wagon, press-ganged into a starring role as a vaudeville clown. Despite the lateness of the hour, work began at once to effect the transition from freight to showpiece. Once more, and inevitably, the operation was conducted under the gaze of a huge, incredulous crowd, even though all that was visible of the whale itself was a corner of its tail that the tarpaulin didn't quite cover. Yet such was the pulling power and fame of the animal that even under a tarpaulin in the dark and on the last night of January on what is routinely the coldest coast in Scotland, they came to stand and stare and try to believe the evidence of their eyes. The operation took 12 hours. The whale, still in its cradle, was jacked up and suspended in mid air (not for the first time in its life after death) so that the railway wagons could be removed. Two road-going wagons were backed into place beneath it, and because the whale had shed 11 tons since the surgical operation (not to mention the loss of its tongue), the wagons survived intact when the whale was lowered again, though the Dundee squad supervising the operation must have had a worrying 'Victoria Dock moment' as the wagons took the strain.

The streets of Aberdeen groaned under the passage of heavy machinery as the whale formed the centrepiece of yet another bizarre convoy behind 30 more horses and another industrial bogie from the Hall-Russell ship yard, a wagon full of logs, rollers and other traditional whale-moving equipment. The journey from the station to the recreation ground took two more hours, then a new variation of the unloading process deposited the whale on a raised platform in front of one more grandstand inside a marquee. The harpoons that killed it – eventually – were also on show (you would expect nothing less in an extravaganza so utterly devoid of taste), as was the seal 'which has been trained to go through a performance of a novel and somewhat interesting character', which endorsement carries more than a hint of damnation by faint praise. Twenty thousand Aberdonians coughed up for the privilege of seeing this shabbiness in just five days.

As I was piecing together the events that defined the fate of the Tay Whale, I found myself thinking time after time that surely my home city couldn't find yet another insult to throw at it. But now I believe that that journey, with its unwieldy logistics, its colossal labour, the ego of the ringmaster, the vaguely unsavoury aspect of one city showing off its dead whale to its near rival, and the grim parody of the whale that was bathed in its lurid Victorian spotlight . . . all that amounted to the worst taunt of all. The whale itself, alive and in good health and well fed on the bounties of that season, could have accomplished the journey by the simple exercise of its tail muscle, and put on such a show for the gatherings of the coast folk on every headland and harbour wall between Dundee and Aberdeen that everyone who saw it would have gasped with a kind of primitive wonder. The whale could have accomplished the journey in a few hours, and having strutted its stuff in the mouth of the Dee for the benefit of the city of Aberdeen, it could have turned again, north for the Atlantic Ocean off Norway, then west, singing and receiving the songs of its kin.

So I started again, with the whale alive and well and unharpooned in the Tay estuary off Newport on the Fife shore, and I rolled a film of a different journey in my head.

Chapter 12

Northward Ho! Take 2

The Dolphin is an animal without malice, living to
be a hundred years old, loving music and friendly to
man.

Konrad of Megenberg
Das Buch der Natur, 1475

Dolphins have a great capacity for altruistic activity.
Anton van Helden, dolphin expert,
in news report of a dolphin that rescued
a beached whale, New Zealand, 2008

I have in my mind's eye nature's plan for the Tay
Whale when its foray in the estuary was done, an
alternative itinerary for the journey to Aberdeen and
beyond once she had prompted the whale into belated
recognition of its predicament. Men in boats armed
with harpoons formed no part of nature's assessment
of that predicament; such things were not predictable
and moved outwith and independently of nature's
sphere of influence in those matters. Rather, those
forces that shaped the whale's awareness of its actions
and its surroundings homed in on the shallowness of

the estuary compared to the open ocean, the speed and impact of the ebb that conspired with a treachery of midstream and offshore sandbanks to constrict a safe channel downstream for a swimming whale. Of course the whale had negotiated many such journeys already under its own steam and without any prompting, but each time it had turned again with the flowing tide, back up the estuary. It seemed that the longer the whale lingered so far up the estuary in pursuit of such an abundant and constantly renewing food source, the more its awareness dulled. Nature's plan was to stimulate the whale to encourage it back to the open sea, and from there to the northern ocean, and from there to the endlessly deepening waters of all the world's oceans as only the whales know them, the singing homeland of the humpback.

The whale lies for an idle hour between the Middle Bank and Pluck the Crow Point, a quarter of a mile off the Fife shore, slack water, the tide full. The whale barely moves, it matches the river's mood, whale and river at rest. Some quality in the late afternoon midwinter light puts violet and navy blue tones in the gleaming curve of its back. A hundred people are gathered here and there along the shore, pointing, gesturing, pronouncing and swapping theories, arguing, or just watching, just marvelling at the monster in their midst. Some have been coming every day for six weeks, making notes, sketches, legends. None is indifferent to the whale. Some wish it dead, some wish it God speed.

The moment is subdued, but the south-west sky has the same dark whale shades in it and begins to advance so that the low hills of north Fife shrink and blur and shrivel beneath its widening, darkening mass.

The river stirs, it crinkles and ripples. A small wave slaps a shoreline rock. The river shakes itself, stretches like a wolf awakening from a doze, and prepares to go to work. The whale is unmoved. It feels the river stir and knows its meaning. It feels the growing tug of the ebb but it stays. The small crowd on the bank is well enough versed in the ways of the estuary's tides, for they affect almost every aspect of life. They know tides, they know boats, they know the comings and goings of seabirds. They do not know whales, not at first hand. They've all heard the whalers' stories, of course, the second-hand exploits of the spring and summer whales in Arctic waters, but this is the winter whale, in their home waters, and they watch and wonder and wager, and not for the first time, it baffles them. An hour after the tide has turned, nothing has changed, except that the Middle Bank has begun to uncover, and to look not unlike a slumbering whaleback itself.

Some of the watchers on the south shore begin to voice concern. Is the whale stuck? Has it grounded? Is it ill? Is it dead? Surely such a stillness is unnatural, especially when the tide is an hour into the ebb? Then quite suddenly it sinks. A 40-foot-long whale vanishes before disbelieving eyes in five seconds. Almost at once it resurfaces and blows, but it has travelled 50 yards upstream. The watchers mutter among themselves: surely *upstream* is wrong? Day after day for weeks (apart from its mysterious ten-day disappearance) the whale has fished the river and turned with the tide, heading for the open sea. The lighthouse keepers out at the Bell Rock look out for it an hour or two after the tide turns. As often as not they confirm its appearance to the harbour authorities in Dundee, and first the newspapers and then (when the newspapers began to weary of such monotonously recurring detail) the grapevine that flows through such places regular as tides brings the news.

But today the whale is drowsy with herring and the ease of its situation, and it edges upstream against the suck of the river. Then it sinks again. Then one of the watchers sees the dorsal fin, points. The humpback dorsal fin is small and low-slung and inconspicuous, but this dorsal fin is none of these. A second watcher thinks its shape has changed, and besides it cuts through the water much too quickly.

'That's not . . .' begins the second watcher, and at that the water opens to permit the airborne shape of a bottlenose dolphin '. . . a whale!' he finishes amid much laughter. If only we lived as long as a humpback whale

139

does, he and his delighted friends would still be talking today about what happens next.

The whale is stationary on the surface again. The dolphin is 100 yards away and apparently closing in on the whale. It leaps again in a black and gleaming curve, the whale blows, the river ebbs flat out, the crowd of watchers thrills and feels its throat tighten. Then its ears hear the exuberant voice as the dolphin flies a yard above the waves, as though a child cries for the sheer joy of living. At that moment the whale turns towards the sound. The whale has heard it too, spins in its own length and blows a plumed greeting a dozen feet in the air, a fine white spray that shreds eastwards on the breeze.

The dolphin rolls across the bow of the whale and dives, resurfaces a few yards upstream. The whale lies on the surface, motionless again but now facing north across the tidal pull, its tail to the crowd on the shore. One eye watches the dolphin. Again the watchers hear the dolphin's voice. Some of them try calling back:

'Oo wee yow ee . . .'

Laughter drowns the mimicry. The dolphin has put a high good humour on their vigil. But if it sees and hears them – and it must – it pays them no attention. They see the whale wheel. It turns to face upstream again, but the dolphin zig-zags a few feet in front of it, apparently trying to block its path – the 10-foot dolphin, the 40-foot, 26-ton whale, the whale that could toss the dolphin 20 feet in the air or swipe it 20 feet sideways across the waves. But it is the dolphin that makes physical contact. It charges the whale (all the watchers agree – it *charges*!) and butts at speed into the upper jaw with its snout. The watchers are unaware that the dolphin uses this technique to drive off sharks, but the whale is unmoved. So the dolphin swims alongside it, swims past its eye, puts its snout against the whale's flank and pushes. The watchers, entranced and (at least here and there among them) mindful of the wonder of what they watch, suddenly realise what is going on. The dolphin is trying to turn the whale! Nature has decided to try and persuade the whale to head downstream and towards the open sea, and she has sent a dolphin, for such rescue and path-finding skills are in the nature of dolphins and are made readily available to seafarers in trouble, whether whale or whaler.

So the dolphin leans its snout into the massive amid-ships of the whale, and shoves; the whale permits the manoeuvre and begins to rotate in its own length until it faces downstream; the dolphin leaps forward beyond the snout of the whale and swims away east.

Follow!

A hundred yards downstream the dolphin stops, turns to see the whale still anchored in the same place, swims back upstream and repeats every detail of the process, the upstream zig-zags, the charge, the head-butt, the snout-amidships shove, the follow-me swim down the firth. This time, the whale sinks as it waves (as the now entranced watchers choose to interpret it) a slow farewell. When it resurfaces it is right on the tail of the dolphin, east-making.

The tide is a big one, one which will ebb to an exceptional low-water mark. There is a channel deep enough to accommodate the swimming whale, and the dolphin navigates it at speed. The whale feels the wisdom of its summons. The whale is suddenly uneasy in the face of that conspiracy of current and ebb tide and sand. The whale does not belong between the walls of the firth. The whale suddenly craves the landless ocean depths, the curving ocean horizon, the vast and curving sky. The whale hears the dolphin's voice chattering back through the water, sound waves that slice a path westward through the salt estuary waves against their eastward march. The meaning of the chatter, crudely translated, is this:

Follow.

The river has treated you well.

Now you must leave.

Otherwise the wildness and wisdom of whales
    will desert you.

The easy living is a deception.

Follow this dolphin's wake.

Follow until you can hear the song of your
    own kind again.

142

The dolphin turns briefly north to pass the grey rocks of the Sea Craig and the Craig Head, then east again round Greenside Scalp, Larick Scalp and past the Pile Lighthouse off Tayport, where the shores of the estuary lean closest, a little less than a mile between the harbours of Tayport and Broughty Ferry. There are, inevitably, more watchers around Broughty Ferry Castle. It has always been the landlubber classes' favourite viewing platform throughout the whale's stay, simply because the river is so narrow here, and at times the whale put on a show for them not 200 yards offshore. The regulars at the castle have their favourite stances which they defend vigorously against occasional or first-time visitors. They also take a proprietorial interest in *their* whale's comings and goings, its adventures and misadventures. Now their interest is stirred again. What's this? There, just ahead of the whale, fussing over it like a collie with a not wholly compliant ewe – it's a dolphin!

They have heard the whalers' dolphin stories, of course. There was the dolphin that piloted the fog-blind whaling ship through pack-ice channels and a moving maze of ice floes to open water and known landmarks. There was the dolphin that saved floundering whalers (traditionally, whalers never learned to swim, a perverse superstition) when their boat capsized close to an ice floe; each whaler was buoyed up and shoved onto the ice one at a time, and deposited face-down and in a heap, not fully understanding why they were still alive.

Fellow crewmen on the mother ship who rescued them and who had seen the whole thing unfold told them what had happened.

And now, here is their whale, heading seawards once more on the ebb as it has done so often before, but this time it appears that a dolphin is leading it. Even as they watch, the whale sinks (there is the slow last flourish of the tail, like a grave salutation for the benefit of all who watch), then . . .

'It's coming up . . .'

. . . The heart-stopping showpiece, the whale lunges for the airspace above its known world, throws one flipper high in the air, twists and crash-lands on its back, then a few seconds later the sound of the splash-down reaches them and they all cheer in spite of themselves, for this is what has underpinned their affection for what they still call 'the monster'. Then again . . . then again . . . four times . . . five, six, seven . . .

And as their own excitement subsides, one in the crowd says quietly, 'It's taking a bow. It's leaving. That's why the dolphin . . .'

His voice trails away, then another voice, much louder this time, 'Three cheers for the whale, hip hip . . .'

And the chorused hoorays are cries of joy, but there is a lacing of threnody in the raised voices too, a keening edge. Then a silence, and every eye strains to see the whale diminish among the waves until finally there is the far-off raised tail and the final dive.

Dolphin and whale pass Lucky Scalp and Green Scalp. (Scalp – 'scaup' as the Fifers might have it – is a sand bank where you find shellfish between high- and low-water marks; this coast was named by the old and practically inclined Scots tongue.) Almost at once, the estuary doubles in breadth, but almost at once the shores also thrust wide plains of sand far into the estuary. So at low tide, south-eastward-and-seaward-looking, the view from, say, the Lady Bank off Barnhill on the north shore is more sand and mud than deep water, for the Abertay Sands are also laid bare and these are miles-long and seal-encrusted, forming an arm, wrist and hand that points to the Bell Rock and Holland, no matter that the pointing hand is called the Elbow; and the sky has grown, and you begin to get the gist of the scope of the sea that lies beyond it all.

The Abertay Lightship sits beyond the Elbow – there is nothing here in this land-and-seascape substantial enough to build a lighthouse on, no fragment of land that stays in one place long enough. Dolphin and whale pass the lightship to the north, and on the north shore Buddon Ness and its two lighthouses are already behind them, and these are the frontier posts of the estuary. They have made the open sea, and nature has reclaimed the humpback from the domain of men.

The coast slews away north, then north-east. South,

there is no longer a coast. But the dolphin holds an easterly course. The whale follows, heeding nature's command at last, and there grows in its mind a longing for the sound of whale song, a thirst for the ocean and an awareness of what it will take to slake that thirst.

Darkness does not halt their progress. The low star of the Bell Rock has glittered since dusk, but now its brightening beam begins its night-long prowl of the waves. The whale knows it for a friend and responds to its beckoning light. But the dolphin is suddenly alongside the whale's snout, leaning against it while they swim. It darts away, turns and crosses the whale's bows in a low, leaping arc from south to north. The whale still leans towards the light. The dolphin dives beneath the whale, and appears a few yards in front of it, and begins to zig-zag again, blocking its path to the light, and as it lines up to launch the kind of charge that turned the whale 20 miles back, between the Middle Bank and Pluck the Crow Point, the whale finally breaks free of the spell of the estuary and its teeming fish shoals and its landmark lighthouse, and turns its back on them all. The dolphin leads the whale slowly north.

The full moon rises, the sea glitters and grows calm. The whale floats on the surface. The sounds are these: two miles to the west, the surf breaks around three red sandstone rock stacks – the Brithers – that mark the entrance to the small natural harbour of East Haven; a skein of whooper swans, Icelanders restlessly wintering between Orkney and the Tay, calls in 20 voices, soft syllables of muted brass, flying above the coast and under the moon, following the ragged white furrow of the surf; a raft of scoters 100-strong, night-black sea-birds, riding the sea, diving to feed, serenades the moonlight with croons and soft growls. The sea slaps softly against the whale, which sleeps, and snores hugely.

In the grey North Sea dawn, the whale has been swimming north for an hour. The dolphin has gone, though it still swims in the memory of the whale, and its urging still determines the whale's course. The harbour of Arbroath and its fishing fleet is unroused. The landmarks of the coast slip by – Whiting Ness, the Needle E'e, the Deil's Heid, Maiden Castle, Lud Castle, Meg's Craig, Maiden Stane, Maw Skelly (not named for a woman but a thrust of rock favoured by gulls – maws or maas), Prail Castle, the unblemished sands of Lunan Bay, Bodding Point, Black Craig, Long Craig, Rashick Knap, Sillo Craig, Scurdie Ness, where the whale sees the lighthouse smoor its lamp for the daylight hours. A fishing boat thrusts a small bow-wave into the sunrise at Montrose; others follow behind, ranged line astern up the narrow estuary of the South Esk. A steam tug, the *Storm King,* is moored and unsummoned in the harbour.

A small fishing boat plies the waters ten miles south-east of Gourdon under a smother of gulls. No one remembers her name. With her stern drift net raised, four oarsmen edge her into sun. By the time they sight the whale, the whale has been watching them for half an hour, has responded to an implanted notion to give her a wide eastward berth. The whale remembers the dolphin again, so strong was the sense of a command to lean to the east.

The skipper sees the whale blow.

'Whale lads, starboard bow!'

They follow the line of his telescope.

'Shall we catch her for supper, skipper?'

'Aye, we can drape a rope round her bottom jaw and tow her home. She'll be gentle as a milk cow.'

And they smirk and then they put their backs to the job in hand, for they have smaller fish to fry this morning.

Away north, the whale sees the long lines of red cliffs in the west, and the villages, each with a harbour, each sustained by the sea alone – Gourdon itself, hard under its own cliff; Catterline's string of clifftop houses. Then Dunnottar Castle high on its sea-girt plinth, a forge of more than its fair share of Scottish history – and English history for that matter, for the castle changed hands endlessly. The Dunnottar that Wallace took from the English in 1296 was not this one (which is an all-but-700-years-old upstart), but its immediate predecessor, and God alone knows how old that was, though perhaps there was a passing whale who saw it rise and fall within its own lifetime. Then, Stonehaven, its beach loud with seabirds where a fish merchant is discarding a too-long-dead fish carcase he knows he will never be able to sell.

The whale wavers once, at the sight of Aberdeen crouched round its harbour. It feels the surge of fresh water out into the sea from the Dee estuary, bounds forward towards the source in a series of 20 crashing breaches, a headlong procession that takes it to within a mile of the sea wall. Long before that, its antics have been spotted from the harbour, and a small crowd of watchers gathers to point and exclaim and stand and stare and wonder. An old hauled-out mariner with his share of whaling years behind him gives the 50 or so watchers the benefit of his wisdom:

'Watch and remember this! Nothing but a humpback puts on a show like this. She's a long way from home, though, shouldn't be any nearer to these waters than the west coast of Norway, and west of Greenland suits her better these days. Word has it there's been one in the Tay at Dundee these last few weeks, and maybe this is she, and she's come to her senses before they run her through with a harpoon just for the hell of it. Not that she's worth the killing, but you know what they're like in Dundee, eh?'

There are few things they enjoy more in Aberdeen

and Dundee than making jokes at each other's expense. A voice in the crowd asks:

'So you wouldn't harpoon her then, Skipper?'

'She's not worth getting wet for! Not enough blubber to light my kitchen for a fortnight and she sinks when she dies. Greenland right whales, now, they're the ones to kill; you can put your arm through the blubber right up to your shoulder and your hand still hasn't come out the other side. And kill her and she sits on the surface and waits for you.

'No, no . . . you wouldn't kill a humpback. And just look at her! Did you ever see anything more agreeable in all nature than that? Look, she's even waving at you. Why would you want to kill such a beast?'

And he waves back with a far-off look in his eyes, and the rest of the crowd find they are waving too, despite themselves. The Skipper speaks again, this time sounding as if he's talking to himself:

'She sings too, you know.'

The whale lies on the surface and blows. The sound reaches the ears of the watchers. The whale, whose mind has been full these last few minutes of a memory of herring shoals trapped in shallow water and fast ebbs and a low star in the sky that blinked to a known rhythm, suddenly recognises a face in the water a few feet ahead, a zig-zagging face. Then it charges and rams the whale amidships. The whale acknowledges the thrust and turns to the north-east, and the red cliffs of the east coast of Scotland sink down into the sea forever. A hundred yards ahead of him, beckoning like a low star in the sky, the arched back and dorsal fin of the dolphin head for the ocean west of Norway.

Back at the sea wall in Aberdeen, the skipper has begun a long story about how a dolphin once led his ship to safety through a conspiracy of fog and pack ice and ice floes to open water and known landmarks.

The next day, news reaches Professor Struthers of Aberdeen University about the visit of the whale to Aberdeen's home waters. He is characteristically dismissive:

'Didn't you kill it? A living whale's no damned good to me. Get me a dead one I can work on, and I'll get excited.'

Chapter 13

Jonah

The 'Tay Whale', which afforded so much sport to the
Philistines while in life, bids fair to yield even a greater
measure of entertainment now that it is only a carcase.
After having been publicly exhibited in Dundee and
Aberdeen, the unwieldy monster has been brought to
Glasgow, and for the next few days it will be on view
. . . On arrival at College Station this morning, the
whale was placed on a large carriage specially con-
structed for the purpose. The carriage, drawn by 30 or
40 horses, proceeded along Ingram Street . . .

Glasgow newspaper report, February 1884

After Aberdeen, the whole circus packed up and headed
for Glasgow, where, as the above newspaper extract
suggests, cynicism was rife. Yet another carriage 'specially constructed for the purpose' was made available –
the third, and there must have been two more in Liverpool and Manchester. Its arrival in Glasgow was
greeted with less than open arms, and the local press's
attitude centred pretty specifically on hygiene. One
mightily relieved reporter anticipated its arrival thus:
'We are assured that the preservation of the carcase has

been so satisfactory that there is now no trace of an unpleasant odour, and that the most delicate or sensitive individual may visit the blubbery cetacean without fear of being distressed.'

So that's all right then. We wouldn't want delicate and sensitive Glaswegian souls being distressed. And there was surely not much chance now of further distressing the whale. Nothing untoward could happen to it now, no further indignities could be heaped on its monstrous reputation; surely there were no more indignities left to heap. But then, on 8 February, the man from the *Advertiser* on an away-day to Glasgow, stumbled on this:

THE TAY WHALE
ASTOUNDING DISCOVERY!
A MAN FOUND IN THE STOMACH!
(By Extra Special Wire)

Glasgow, 2p.m.
Extraordinary excitement prevails in Glasgow owing to the discovery this forenoon of a live man in the stomach of the Tay whale. The stomach, and over three tons of intestines were sent from Aberdeen a week ago under the direction of Professor Struthers, but it was only today that preparations had been completed for the opening of the stomach. A number of the University Professors and other scientific gentlemen were present by invitation, as

153

also several clergymen and prominent citizens. About noon a large incision was made, and the stomach partially opened, when something in the nature of a solid obstruction was encountered. Curiosity changed into utter amazement when, on the incision being enlarged and the upper portions of the stomach being carefully drawn back, the obstruction was found to be a human being, lying in an easy position, as in sleep, with the body bent; with the right arm, which was underneath, doubled at the elbow; and the side of the nose resting on the forefinger. It was supposed at first that the man was dead, but on closer investigation by the medical men present it was discovered that he was actually alive, but in a torpid or comatose state resembling catalepsy. Besides the man, the stomach contained scores of dead herring and sprats, and several articles of different kinds, including a large pocket-book and the glass funnel of an oil lamp (blackened with smoke) exactly similar to those used in the Tay Ferry steamers.

It was thought prudent not to extricate the sleeping figure until the procurator-fiscal could be summoned; but attempts were made to waken him up by shouting. The Rev. John Smith, who was present, succeeded, with the assistance of two other gentlemen, in so bending over as to get his mouth close to the sleeper's ear; but though he shouted at the pitch of his voice, not the slightest effect was produced . . .

So far, so very bizarre, but then the Rev. Mr Smith took leave of his senses:

> Mr Smith expressed his conviction in the most solemn and emphatic manner, that the man was no other than the prophet Jonah, and that the whale and the unfaithful prophet had both been preserved miraculously, and been directed to these shores as a triumphant refutation of modern scepticism.

You can almost hear the whale groaning, 'Why me, God?'

The astounding bit about what followed is that several people in the assembled multitude actually took issue with the Rev. Smith on matters of biblical accuracy rather than convulsing into helpless laughter then having him incarcerated as an irredeemable lunatic. They pointed out that the whale that ate Jonah then vomited him out onto dry land. Don't think Mr Smith hadn't seen that one coming. Jonah, he said, must have deserted his post again and been swallowed again.

> He appealed, somewhat excitedly, to all present, whether there was any record either in the Bible or in natural history of any other whale having a throat large enough to swallow a man, except the one that swallowed Jonah. It had been specially created to swallow him when he was

refusing to attend to his duty, and was no doubt kept in readiness to swallow him in like circumstances again.

Alas for Mr Smith's revisionist theories of both the Bible story and the natural world that had apparently sustained a whale (and Jonah) for the better part of 2,000 years so that God in His wisdom might spectacularly confound his doubting Thomases, the sleeper was recognised as a tramp and general pain-in-the-arse who haunted the Tay Ferries that plied between Dundee and Newport.

At this moment, Mr William Sanderson, of Newport, Fife, who had been superintending the exhibition of the outer carcase of the whale, having heard of the extraordinary discovery that had been made, arrived, and no sooner saw the sleeper than he declared, to the astonishment of all present, that it was a gentleman from his own part of the country, unpopularly known as the Autocrat of the Tay Ferries. He knew the face perfectly. He was prepared to take affidavit that this was the man.

So not Jonah, then. Damn.

Several men contradicted Mr Sanderson and suggested that the pocketbook might identify the man, although why they thought the book might be a more reliable source than Mr Sanderson is not explained. The man from the *Advertiser* was now clearly beginning to enjoy himself.

On the pocket book being opened it was found to contain a large number of musty papers which did not appear to have been touched in a long time. As the first scrap was being opened, the Rev. Mr Smith, who adhered firmly to his conviction that the man was Jonah, expressed his opinion from the faded appearance of the paper, that it would prove to be a Tarshish or Nineveh bank-note. On closer examination, however, it was found to be an account for 'ten gallons of inferior oil for saloon'. A note in the corner of this account read as follows: 'This kind has a very bad smell, but is one ha'penny per gallon cheaper.'

The next thing brought out was a printed slip, containing maxims and mottoes such as 'How not to do it', 'Procrastination is the soul of business', and 'Never do tomorrow what you can let alone today'. There was also a tract entitled 'Official indifference a saving grace'. Several little scraps of manuscript were next brought out. On these being carefully unfolded, it was found that most of them had headings as of topics to write about or consider. Amongst these were the following: 'Patience a valuable virtue – ferry – for the public', 'How to sit upon other Ferry Trustees', 'How best to provoke patient people', 'How to keep saloon passengers from knowing when the gangway is down', 'How to attain the maximum of smell with the minimum of speed'. There were also some jottings under the heading, 'Advantages of carrying people and cattle in the same boat' . . . The only other contents were letters, all of which were found to be complaints. Several were dated months, even years ago. None of them seemed to have been opened.

LATER DETAILS, 3 P.M.

The question of identification being still unsettled, a messenger has been sent off to wire Dundee and Newport. The opinion of some is that the pocket-book may have no connection with the man, and may have been swallowed by the whale at a different time and place. Mr Sanderson, however, adheres to his first assertion . . .

You had a feeling he would, didn't you?

Meantime, more vigorous efforts have been made to get the sleeper roused. Two powerful batteries of sixteen horse power have been applied, but without producing the slightest effect. The doctors have made a further examination and report that the structure and condition of the sleeper are both remarkable. The pulsation and everything else is exceptionally slow; and the bump of Aggravativeness covers the entire area usually occupied by the moral faculties. Guns are to be fired this afternoon close to the exposed ear; but the doctors doubt if they will produce any movement or response.

They didn't. And there, infuriatingly, the sleeper vanishes from the story, his fate unrecorded. Perhaps the guns fired close to his exposed ear were poorly aligned and shot him in the head by mistake? A centenary leaflet produced by Dundee Art Galleries and Museums in 1984 simply notes that 'although some commentators claimed the man to be a modern Jonah, and a sign from God, a Newport man recognised the sleeper as a tramp who regularly frequented the Tay Ferries. It was presumed that he had crawled into the whale's mouth while it had been stationary at a railway yard in Dundee in transit.'

But that won't do. The stomach was removed at Greasy Johnny's yard on 25 January and popped into a barrel to be freighted to Aberdeen, barrels having been established as the means by which body parts were freighted. By the time the stomach was opened in Glasgow, on February 8, the tramp had been inside the stomach for at least a fortnight. But how did he manage to enter the stomach in the first place, bearing in mind that the professors had to cut it open to reveal the contents? Did he enter the whale's mouth when it first came home to Dundee (as so many others did to have their photographs taken) and just kept going to find somewhere warm? Or did he fall off the ferry into the Tay while the whale was still alive just as the whale was passing with its mouth open? Good heavens, the poor fellow could have been harpooned in there! Now that would have been a truly remarkable way to die.

They mystery died with the tramp, and the tramp almost certainly died within a day or two of his discovery, and however he died it was a truly remarkable death.

Yet the incident has its echoes elsewhere in the history of whaling. David Jones notes in his book, simply called *Whales*:

In 1891 a whaler, James Bartley, published his first-hand account of how a whale saved him – albeit the hard way – from drowning. According to Bartley, he fell overboard and hadn't even hit the water before a sperm whale swallowed him. Bartley's shipmates caught the whale within the hour and began butchering it. When they cut open the stomach, out spilled Bartley, his hair and skin bleached a deathly white by the whale's gastric juices. After two weeks in a coma, Bartley made a complete recovery but stayed an albino for the rest of his days. Most authorities today dismiss the account as a hoax, arguing it would be impossible for a person to survive more than a few minutes in a whale's stomach.

Perhaps that explains the Tay Whale sleeper too – a hoax. Perhaps the subsequent newspaper silence reflects embarrassment – they were hoodwinked and they didn't like it. Perhaps it really happened and perhaps (the smell apart) the stomach of a dead whale is a warm and comparatively comfortable bivvy, especially for a tramp on a cold January night. Maybe he too recovered after a couple of weeks in a coma to haunt the Fifies (which is how all Dundee affectionately referred to the Tay Ferries right up to the days of their demise in the 1960s, when the road bridge rendered them redundant) with his ghostly whale-pallor for years to come. But I think we would have heard.

The rest of the whale's tour – to Manchester and Liverpool – passed off without drama. It was finally transported back to Aberdeen, where the skull and remaining bones were removed (it took six men to carry the skull), the skeleton's component parts were reunited, cleaned and generally made acceptable for public consumption, transported back to Dundee where they were delivered to the city's Albert Institute museum (subsequently the McManus Galleries) and reassembled in the right order, and put on more or less permanent display. More or less permanent, because in 1983 the skeleton was moved a few hundred yards to the smaller Barrack Street museum, but not before several Dundee councillors had protested at the cost of moving a heap of old bones, and one suggested having it ground down to make dog food as a means of recouping some of the expense it had incurred over the years. Fifteen years later it returned to the McManus, and as I write, the McManus Galleries are being refurbished (the whale will form the centrepiece of a new exhibit on Dundee at work) and the skeleton is being stored in pieces in various parts of the city, and that, too, has happened before. It never was allowed to rest in peace.

In the intervening 125 years, public attitudes to whales and whaling have been transformed. The fate of the Tay Whale was a product of its time, even though many of those who saw it alive would rather it had stayed that way. The Victorians' attitude to nature was one of subjugation; to command it, kill it, skin it, stuff it, mount it and show it off, or if it was to be spared, then it was to live in zoos, in circuses, and commanded to do tricks. Greasy Johnny was the archetypal Victorian ringmaster. His next venture into the business was announced in a newspaper advertisement in 1886:

LAST WEEK OF THE BEARS!
Positively closing on Saturday 6th February
TO BE SEEN ALIVE
AT COMMERCIAL STREET (top of Seagate)
THE THREE LARGEST POLAR BEARS
EVER IMPORTED from the ARCTIC REGIONS

These Beautiful Animals, which are as White as the driven Snow, were brought to Dundee by the Brothers, Captains Fairweather, in the whale ships 'Arctic' and 'Terra Nova', and will be Exhibited here for a few days only, previously to being sent to the

Zoological Gardens, Dublin. Mr Woods, wishing
the inhabitants of Dundee to have an opportunity
of seeing them, has decided to make the Price of
Admission merely nominal. ONLY 2d.

On view from 9 a.m. to 10 p.m.

The other notable characteristic of Victorian attitudes
to wild animals is, alas, not yet wholly extinct in Scotland. It is that if one species of nature was found to
conflict with the vested interests of people's pursuit of
another species of nature, then the one interfering
species was eradicated – the eagle that hunted over
the grouse moor, for example, could not be permitted
to kill grouse. It had to be killed so that the people could
kill the grouse.

I believe that in the Victorian era we grew retarded as
a race because of that perverse relationship with nature.
It feels now – some of the time at least – as if we have
begun to reverse the process, as if we are taking the first
tentative steps across a bridge, a bridge that reconnects
us with all the possibilities of nature, not just the ones
we find convenient; a bridge that reconnects us with
who and what we used to be and with who and what we
should have remained all along. There are an infinite
number of steps on that bridge, and it may yet break
with the weight of expectation on it. Yet we heal as we
cross, and as we heal, nature heals.

Beyond the bridge's further end there are well-wooded mountains, clear rivers and unpolluted seas. If my forebears in Dundee had admired the Tay Whale when it turned up, and watched sorrowfully when it left but felt gratitude for his visit, then it could have been alive to see the first steps along the bridge, alive and singing as it travelled the oceans of the world.

Chapter 14

The First Whale

People simply don't forget the first time in their lives
that they saw a whale. They never say to you, 'Well, I
just can't remember whether I've seen a whale or not.'
(Or if they do, you know they haven't seen one.)

Roger Payne
Among Whales

My first whale? Killer.

Mid June 1988, 4 a.m., en route from St Kilda to
Tobermory on Mull, eight hours out of St Kilda, three
hours out from Tobermory, the Skye Cuillin looking
strangely misplaced in the north-east, Coll and Tiree
low-slung blue hulls in the south-east and more or less
dead ahead.

I had been camping on St Kilda for two weeks,
researching what would become my first book. Transport arrangements for the return journey to far-off
Scotland and the known world were sketchy, so when
it was suggested to me by the island's warden that
I might hitch a lift on the handsome two-masted
schooner *Jean de la Lune,* a seasoned St Kilda voyager,

I accepted his advice. I had had a charmed stay on St Kilda, I had filled notebooks, piled typewritten pages in a corner of the tent (and some had been nibbled by St Kilda's famous field mouse, as had four Bounty bars, three apples, a packet of soup, two holes in the tent and one in a rucksack; little wonder the wee bugger's an endangered species), taken a hundred photographs, scribbled a dozen sketches, walked and walked and walked, and I had more or less decided it was time to take what I had home and make sense of it. I struck camp quickly and headed down to the shore, where I met the skipper. I remember his affable greeting:

'Got any Stugeron?'

'Yes. In my pack.'

'Well start poppin' 'em.'

He had just heard the weather forecast and it promised boisterousness. I thought wistfully of my crossing from South Uist in the big Army flat-bottomed landing-craft, a brute with a fearsome reputation among St Kilda veterans. 'It wallows like a drunken pig', I was assured. I had never seen a drunken pig, but it was obviously an image calculated to terrify. Its explicit message was, 'You are going to suffer.' I didn't. I had got chatting to a stranger in the Dark Island Hotel, famed Lochboisdale watering hole among St Kilda travellers, and he turned out to be something senior at the missile tracking station on St Kilda. He insisted

The First Whale

I spend the crossing with him in the officer's mess, and I was wined and dined in mid ocean. Better still, I had the nearest thing anyone will ever experience on that crossing to a flat calm. I was roused at 5 a.m. by a crewman shouting:

'Anyone want to see St Kilda? It's worth a look.'

So I went out on deck, rubbing sleep from my eyes, and St Kilda's cut-out island shapes stood unforgettably erect from a pink sea like an improbable stage set, and it was purple, and it was worth a look.

The *Jean de la Lune* had been chartered by a party of divers when I boarded for the journey home, so I had no berth, but then hitch-hikers don't expect berths. Instead, I stood in the stern watching St Kilda diminish and slip below the horizon over several enchanted hours, and my leave-taking was escorted by wave-top skeins of gannets and thousands and thousands of ticker-tape puffins. The notebook in my hand was supposed to accommodate my impressions of the leave-taking. Instead, I thought about the last St Kildans in 1930 as they evacuated what had been their island home for the previous 4,000 years. They were the guardians of a unique species of island-ness, an oceanic isolation 40 miles west of the Western Isles, and whatever might befall St Kilda in the future, something remarkable was instantly and irretrievably lost. A poem stuttered down the page in my hand:

The Winter Whale

The Old Song

To have lived here,
a hovel on Hirta
for your only hearth
(not nomads of science or soldiery
nor passing prowlers with pens
like me or Dr Johnson),
to bide all your times here
knowing no other's march
was to look wilderness in the eye
and dare it to deny
your daily bread.

To have lived here,
content with all the world
in your embrace, at ease
with all its ways,
then hear compatriots whisper
'evacuate!', was to feel
the soul's anchor drag,
to know that whatever the voyage,
wherever the final haven,
the journey was done,
the old song sung.

I had never tasted that kind of ocean place before, never
felt loneliness as a benevolent force before, and I

thought then I would never try and go back because I had been accorded an extraordinary glimpse under the skin of the place and felt dangerously close to it, and now that I too had made my small evacuation, it would be ungracious to ask for it all again. Eventually, about 1 a.m., I dozed off stretched out on a bench in the galley. Then at 4 a.m., the mate's voice from the wheelhouse:

'You still there, Jim?'

'Uh-huh.'

'Come up and see this.'

So I joined him in time to see something shaped like a small Matterhorn crossing the bows about 50 yards away. It was quite black and looked about six feet tall. I said:

'What is it?'

'Killer.'

No other part of the whale showed; no hint of head or back or belly or tail, no suggestion of its brute mass, its tonnage. I thought of a nuclear submarine I once saw steaming south between Skye and the Scottish mainland, only the conning tower above the water, the unnerving silence of it as it steamed through the narrows. It was an ill-fitting and wretchedly inadequate image, but I had been quite unprepared for my first whale, and it was four in the morning after three hours' sleep. But perhaps nothing ever can prepare you for your first whale. There was a half-formed feeling that there should have been more

– perhaps a vast streamlining beneath the boat with adrenalin-pumping closeness (the submarine again); or the all-guns-blazing whoosh of a breaching humpback straight off an Alaskan travel brochure; but certainly more whale, more than that eerie, silent, travelling black cone with no visible means of support or propulsion. Then it was lost among a glittering endlessness of waves, and it was a morning of breathtaking blue beauty, and briefly I had shared it with a piece of a whale.

'People simply don't forget the first time in their lives that they saw a whale. They never say to you: "Well, I can't remember whether I've seen a whale or not."'

No. You never forget your first whale. You never forget the sense of something other. You never forget the feeling of knowing but not seeing that which is hidden, the bulk of what is unrevealed by that glimpse of a dorsal fin, nor the awareness of distance being devoured, nor the notion of a world traveller on the march from ocean to ocean to ocean.

The thing unsettled me. To this day, I remain unsettled by it.

I stayed up on deck after that, helped the mate with the sails while the divers slept through it, slept off their huge last-night meal and last-morning-after hangovers. We nosed into the Sound of Mull, and suddenly the ocean was elsewhere, behind and beyond, and the whale was with it, betrothed to it, wave-cleaving, and the entire worldful of waves lay in wait and at its effortless disposal.

We tied up in Tobermory at 7 a.m. and the sun was already high and warm. I said my goodbyes and thank yous and stepped ashore, and the quayside still moved beneath my feet to the ocean's rhythm. I had two hours to wait for a bus to Craignure and the ferry to Oban. I walked along the coast away from the harbour until I found a rock to sit on where I could stare at the sea. Strange, I thought, this side of the island it's 'the sea', the other side it's 'the ocean'. It's the same water, but it isn't. The thing about St Kilda was that it was all 'the ocean' regardless of which side of the island you walked.

I daydreamed among the flotsam of the last two weeks. I remembered standing on Connachair, the summit of all St Kilda at 1,234 feet, looking out and turning through 360 degrees and seeing no other land at all. There were the jagged thrusts of the St Kilda archipelago, a sparse cluster of bird-tormented rocks, and then, in every direction, only the hypnotic oceanic nothing, which was only a nothing because its scope was incomprehensible, its depths unplumbable in my head. I had chatted the night before with one of the divers, listened to his vivid account of the undersea St Kilda, its colours, creatures, of swimming among hunting puffins, of the rock faces of the familiar overworld shapes that went on down and down into the murk. I briefly envied him that glimpse, but now I know this: that if a blue whale, the world's biggest creature, were to up-end with the tip of its tail on the surface and its head vertically below its tail, its snout would already be at a depth greater than most scuba divers will ever go. And its dive is yet to begin. And if it so chooses, it can dive down to where the island shapes we know are anchored to the raw stuff of the rest of the planet. When all is said and done the ocean is the whale's place, and we scratch its surface and grow sea-sick.

One glimpse of a whale at 50 yards made me reassess my ideas about it, gave it shape, gave it landscape, direction, trade routes, migrations, populations, infinite possibilities; one 30-second glimpse of a whale at 50 yards did that. I can close my eyes and see it now.

'What is it?'

'Killer.'

It is an awful name. Not even 'killer whale', just 'killer'. Even in a good field-guide index you don't find it among the 'w's for 'whale, killer'. You find it among the 'k's, for killer. Of course it kills, they all kill something; and anyway, who are we to talk? Some old hauled-out mariners with the Newfoundland whaling grounds on their CV would have told you the killers used to drive the humpbacks towards the whaleboats making them easier for the whalers to kill, and the killers in the boats and the killers in the waves would share the spoils. But some old hauled-out mariners talked a lot of rot too.

It was named, I suppose, because men – whalers – saw it kill other whales, seals, walruses, penguins, whatever. And if the irony ever occurred to them that their choice of name for it was the worst case of the pot calling the kettle black in the whole vexed history of our relationship with the natural world, they never let it show. And twenty-first-century wildlife documentaries love to show a killer shredding seals in the surf, so we swallow the propaganda whole. Even Gavin Maxwell, a writer of rare genius, whose work was as responsible as anything else for the path my own life would eventually take as a nature writer, was fooled by it. He wrote in *Ring of Bright Water,* 'A killer or two comes every years to Camusfearna, but they do not linger, and if they did I would compass their deaths by any means that I could, for they banish other sea life from my surroundings; also I do not care to be among them in a small boat . . .' This from a man who had killed basking sharks for a living. Herman Melville wrote in the most famous whale book of them all, *Moby Dick,* that 'exception might be taken to the name bestowed upon this whale, on the grounds of its indistinctness. For we are all killers, on land and on sea; Bonapartes and sharks included'.

There are two aspects to the memory of that first whale 20 years ago that strike me now as significant.

One is that I didn't make much of it at the time. It made no appearance in that first book, not so much as an afterthought: oh, by the way, I saw a whale on the way home. But it was the last sensational event of a sensation-crammed adventure, and I suppose it suffered as a result. Perhaps if it had turned up on the outward journey it might have set a different tone for the adventure, given the book more of an ocean-going aspect, whereas the book I wrote remained within the known realm of islands.

Yet the whale's significance to my nature-writing life, and to my constantly evolving relationship with the natural world, cannot easily be overstated. I hoarded it for a year or two, but then as the islands of Scotland's west and north coasts encroached more and more on the mainstream of my work, it acquired a talismanic significance and became the most durable image of the St Kilda voyage. In the greater scheme of things, the story of the St Kildan people (extraordinary as it was) is a trifling episode in the natural history of the place – 4,000 years, and they have been out-lived by mice.

The curious thing about St Kilda is that it is such an introverting place, and not just for visitors; it turned the native people inward, even to the extent that they were notoriously poor sailors (they *rowed* 50 miles to Skye to pay their rents to the MacLeod at Dunvegan, then 50 miles back again), more or less ignored the possibilities of fishing the ocean, and lived largely on seabirds and their eggs. Yet that glimpse of the whale, now that all these things have had time to settle in my mind and assume relative importance and unimportance, was a kind of signpost alerting me to the possibilities of oceans rather than the limitations of islands. They got it wrong, the whale was saying, they should have learned to live on the ocean.

The second aspect of the whale encounter is this: never at any point did I make even the loosest connection between what I had seen out there in the Atlantic somewhere between St Kilda and Tiree and that wretched skeleton suspended from the ceiling of a Dundee museum that was the sum total of my very first exposure to the world of whales. In my young life, the word 'whale' was incomplete without the word 'Tay' in front of it, and it meant a museum piece, static and strung-up and defeated, something you might have made from an Airfix construction kit like a Lancaster bomber, a relic. All you would have needed was an instruction leaflet and enough glue. It occurs to me now that the whole thing was so distasteful in my young mind that it actually set my mind against whales. The museum curators thought they were creating a monument to a way of life, and perhaps it can be argued that they did that well enough. But a child with a love of nature deep inside him from the moment he was able to walk outside alone was repulsed by it, and for 40 years of his life he was denied the possibilities of oceans. I can hardly blame the Victorian curators, of course, or even their heirs who inherited the whale in my own lifetime. They could hardly have foreseen the effects of their curating policies on one child whose life was always going to be more susceptible to the forces of nature than to the example of those dead industrialists who built the city I was born into.

And of course, they weren't to know that I wouldn't meet a living whale on its own terms until I was 41. Life might have dealt me a different hand altogether and our paths might have crossed when I was 21. But as it turned it out, the timing couldn't have been better. I was a newspaper journalist for 24 years, and in the late spring of 1988 I had decided to take the plunge, to try and write what I wanted to write, and when I went to St Kilda with my first publishing contract in my pocket, I was also working my notice. I would leave my last newspaper staff job on 21 October, and *St Kilda* would be published the following day. So it was a heady moment when I set sail for St Kilda and two weeks that effectively changed the course of my life. And with those two astonishing weeks behind me, and a lucky meeting with the warden who suggested that the *Jean de la Lune* might give me a lift home, I set off on another course and crossed the path of a talisman.

'You still there, Jim?'

'Uh-huh.'

'Come up and see this.'
'What is it?'
'Killer.'

So I began to wonder about whales then, and to read up on them, from the most basic whales-of-the-world picture book to good non-fiction and fiction and poetry. One ingredient characterised them all, the one that has always been precious to me as a nature writer – mystery.

'I suspect that the brains of cetaceans have evolved for some very important reason,' wrote Roger Payne, 'about which we haven't a clue, and that dolphins must do some crucially important thing with them, though heaven knows what it is.'

There was so much that people did not know, so much that was wonderfully elusive, and I found that reassuring. I am always reassured when I rub up against some tribe of nature that baffles science. When a scientist like Roger Payne holds up his hands and says 'I haven't a clue', I applaud.

Then I landed a publishing contract with Jonathan Cape in London. It had nothing to do with whales – it was for a book called *A High and Lonely Place* and it was about the Cairngorms, a mountain range as comprehensively landlocked as any in Scotland – but during my first meeting with my editor at Cape he told me about another nature book he was handling, a long poem by Heathcote Williams with a supplementary anthology of short extracts from the copious literature of whales and whaling. This was my introduction to *Whale Nation*. Its impact was substantial. It was incendiary, heaping fuel on the polarised debate surrounding international whaling and fanning the flames of the pro-whale lobby's ardour. The next time I met my editor he handed me a copy of it. Once I had read it, once I had imbibed its potent mix of beauty and anger and its explicit and implicit images, and its mystery, I became an involuntary recruit into the world-wide cause of whales.

When people who do not write for a living meet people who do, they invariably ask about inspiration. The only inspiration I believe in is the example of others. Williams's poem was inspirational. A sample:

> With glowing tracks behind them in the water, large
> as ships',
> The humpbacks use the rotational forces of the planet,
> The azimuth of the sun,
> The taste and temperature of the tides,
> The contours of the sea-bed:
> Canyons, plains, vaults;
> The mountainous summits of the mid-Atlantic ridge,
> twice the width of the Andes,
> Which stretches for ten thousand miles, from Iceland
> to Patagonia;
> Guided by hydrothermal vents in the earth's crust,

The First Whale

The topography of coral reefs,
The position of the moon, and its tidal pull;
Navigating with a lodestone disc made of polarised
    magnetite,
A compass in the brain,
Sensitive to the geomagnetic flow of force-fields
Under phosphorescent seas,
They find their way to the mating grounds.

What nature writer would not want to make the acquaintance of such a beast?

Chapter 15

Up Close and Very Personal

> He is the most gamesome and light-hearted of all
> the whales, making more gay foam and white water
> generally than any other of them.
>
> Herman Melville
> *Moby Dick*, 1851

> . . . what captivates me most about them is their songs.
> During their breeding season, humpback whales pro-
> duce long, complex sequences of sounds that can be
> heard by listening through a hydrophone . . . These
> songs are much longer than birdsongs and can last up
> to thirty minutes, though fifteen is nearer the norm.
> They are divided into repeating phrases called themes.
> When the phrase is heard to change (usually after a few
> minutes), it heralds the start of a new theme. Songs
> contain from two to nine themes and are strung
> together without pauses so that a long singing session
> is an exuberant, uninterrupted river of sound that can
> flow on for twenty-four hours or longer.
>
> Roger Payne
> *Among Whales*

And I have heard the humpback sing. The boat engine
had been cut and the babble of voices, edgy with

adrenalin, had hushed. Suddenly there were only sea sounds, wave-slap, kittiwake cry, an easy breeze that made the flag flap. We were in among the whales and the hydrophone went over the side. The old hands had told us what to expect; the novices, the first-timers, of which I was one, found that the voices of the old hands had too much of the seen-it-all-before to be helpful. I had tried not to listen. I wanted silence, and I wanted the thing, whatever it was, however it sounded, to come at me in its own time out of the silence, out of wherever it came from, however it came. I had thought it might sound a little like jazz: Ellington always had the most animal-like soloists – Harry Carney (baritone sax); Cootie Williams (trumpet); Coleman Hawkins (tenor sax) playing 'Solitude' unaccompanied is the breath of a dark creature at night that might as easily be a whale. Or Sibelius – the wandering clarinet that introduces the first symphony or the throbbing cellos that introduce the sixth, or the pounding figure at the end of the fifth that symbolises swans' wings, but might as easily be whale song set to an ocean rhythm. So I listened, we all listened, and the boat filled up with gales of silence.

A few hours before, my host's car had climbed a steep hill and leaned into a tight bend at the top. Suddenly there was water everywhere far below us, but it was water hemmed in by forested mountains of improbable height and steepness, and every shore was an inlet or a bay or a creek or the end of a glacier. It was not what I had expected of the Pacific Ocean. The car nosed to a standstill and I looked down to where a wide circle of white water suddenly bloomed, and a whale surfaced in its midst. I yelled, I really yelled:

'*LOOK! A WHALE!*'

My host, who really had seen it all before because he lived here, grimaced at the sound of my voice, then said:

'Yep, we got cheap thrills here, Jim.'

'Here' meant Gustavus, a tiny town a stone's throw from Glacier Bay in the south-east of Alaska. It was ten years after St Kilda, ten years after the first whale, and I was embarked on the second life-changing adventure of my writing life, and I had just seen my second whale, and it was a humpback. I was in Alaska to make two radio programmes for the BBC Natural History Unit, programmes about the relationship between people and wilderness, and one of the reasons I was in Gustavus was to see whales. It was a preposterous notion, the idea that you could pick up a phone in Bristol (which is where the NHU is based) and make arrangements to see whales 4,000 miles away in Glacier Bay, Alaska, but that was more or less what my producer had done. I also saw grizzly bears on Kodiak Island, trumpeter swans in the Yukon Territory, sea otters, moose and (very nearly) wolves on the same basis. I was there for three weeks, during which time I travelled constantly, mostly by bush plane, and didn't quite scratch the surface of the surface of Alaska, but it put the taste of northern wilderness in the back of my throat, and a hazy notion between my ears of what Scotland might have looked like and felt like a thousand years ago. And for ten years I have gone back to Alaska in my mind at least once a week.

So the car had stopped, a fragmented corner of the Pacific Ocean had unrolled, and a humpback whale swam in its own maelstrom of white water. From above it seemed to skate over the surface, yet, because the water was so clear, and because I was so high above it, I could see the submerged parts of the animal too, and I saw the tail hoisted from below the surface, saw it burst into the sunlight with water pouring in a brilliant white wall over its trailing edge, saw it hold high and level for a few seconds, saw the whale dive and the tail follow, saw the whale grow dim, and vanish.

> So hurrah! for the mighty monster whale
> That has 17 feet 4 inches from tip to tip of a tail . . .

I measured the room where I am writing this, and it is 16 feet from wall to wall. The tail of a humpback would simply have filled the room and curled round at the edges. It is an absurd observation, except that this is my working environment, and the Pacific Ocean was the working environment of my first humpback, the Pacific and the Atlantic and all the world's other oceans. I know, I have that other working environment beyond the window where I find my raw material and bring it back to the desk in some shape or form, but in 20 years of writing about the natural world for a living, I never crossed the path of a creature with a room-sized tail before or since.

'Ready?'

My host was eager to be moving. There was a boat to catch. I made one last sweep of the water with binoculars, turned back to the car, nodded, climbed in and sat in a kind of stupefied silence.

'Don't worry. There will be other humpbacks. And if you're lucky they'll come to you.'

The boat was an open launch with a wheelhouse and room for about a dozen people to sit, and it was full, and it was full of chatter about whales. We were cautioned against high expectations – not everyone saw whales every day. But they were definitely around and it had been a good week. It was an astounding day of late August, warm (for Alaska), the water calm and fringed with a haze of mountains and forests at almost every compass point, so it felt as if we sailed on an inland sea, rather than an arm of the Pacific.

There was a tension among us that I didn't like, although I undoubtedly contributed to it. A boatful of rising voices, my barely suppressed irritation rising with them, struck me as an unseemly basis on which to go forth and negotiate with whales. Didn't I remember reading something about the old skippers reaching a pact in the early days of the steam whalers to cut their engines and proceed under sail when they were among the whales so that the whales stayed calm and every whaling crew had a chance? Besides, I am instinctively quieter than this, and this small herd of people corralled on a wee boat was taking me over. Then a whale blew.

A thin column of white water rose with a sound like the gust of a fast wind going through tall trees. It was a quarter of a mile away, it rose perhaps a dozen feet in the air then drifted into shapelessness on the breeze. Something like the overturned hull of a longboat appeared on the surface, and two-thirds of the way along it there was a short, backwards-leaning fin. More of the hull appeared, and over a minute it transformed from hull to something distinctly whale-shaped. The boat could not contain itself. Instant cameras craned, automatic flashes popped, and the resultant pictures would show a blurred whale the size of a fly on a bleached ocean. Some serious telephoto lenses were unfurled, but the press of bodies didn't bode well for their possibilities either.

The first difference I noticed between that humpback and my memory of the St Kilda killer was that the humpback did not appear to be going anywhere. It was idling on the surface. The boat inched closer, engines throttled right back. Then there were two whales. Then three. Then six. They loafed close together on the surface. And they did nothing much. Then one turned and lifted its tail clear of the water and my stomach turned over. The tail was black and it shone in the sun and the water poured from it, then the whale went under and the tail slid in without a sound. And the boat said, 'OOOOOOOOOOHHHHHHH-HH!!!!!!!!!!!'

Then there was a pent-up lull. Then the ocean parted. From the space it had made for itself, it threw a whale at the sky. The whale did not get very close to the sky, in fact its tail did not clear the water completely, and at an angle of about 70 degrees it twisted in the air so that its back, which had been facing the sky, now faced the sea. This happened less than 200 yards away. But then there was the most affecting gesture of all. The whale waved. No one had told me about the possibility that the whale might wave to me. No one had mentioned that the humpback's flippers can be anything up to 14 feet long, or that when the ocean threw it at the sky, it would take the time in its brief flight to raise one and wave it at me, a personal salutation, a greeting that consummated our meeting, and that said quite unambiguously how grateful the whale was that I should travel 4,000 miles for the privilege of witnessing that moment. That was what I felt. That was what Roger Payne had in mind when he said that the arrival of a whale along your coast sent a message 'that speaks directly – one capable of setting up waves that propagate right into the core of your very being'. At that moment, with the head and body of the whale poised somewhere between the ocean and the sky, the whale upside-down in the air, and one flipper raised in greeting, the propagating waves had reached so far into the core of my very being that I was having trouble breathing out. Then the whale started to descend, back towards the ocean that had thrown it. The ocean duly caught it. The splashdown was a thunderclap, and where there had been a mid-air whale there was now a geyser, and I felt briefly overwhelmed by this simple show of natural forces. And the boat said, 'OOOOHHHHHWOOOOOOO-WWW!!!!!!!!!'

At every breach and every blow, the boat hurled exclamations at Alaska, and I have no doubt at all that I made my share. It was impossible not to react, not to be as caught in the whales' spell as a herring in a net. The whales drifted closer to the boat in one of their lulls, and they were lazing, and you would have said that they were enjoying the quiet afternoon hour by relaxing at the surface, enjoying the company of other whales, except that you have no more idea what they are doing than the next man, and he is no wiser than you. During the longest lull, I tried to step back and see the whole thing from afar. I tried to be an eagle crossing Glacier Bay a few thousand feet up and looking down. From there I would see the ocean beyond the entrance to the bay, the unfettered Pacific. From there I would see the mountains of Alaska and Canada and the northwestern United States, the unfettered scope of mountains that dismissed notions of national boundaries and recognised only the authority of the ocean as having similar rank to themselves. From there I would see that fringe of ocean and mountain where the creatures of ocean and land met in unequal circumstances, and I was a piece of plankton in the jaws of the world, and that nearest whale was an ambassador for that world-travelling ocean that held the continents together and kept the whole thing round. A whale, when you have time to linger over it and think about what you are seeing, when you have time to hear what it says when it speaks directly and propagates right into the core of your very being, has the capacity to make you rethink yourself and your world. It may be that whales will eventually save the world, even as the world thinks it is trying to save the whales.

Then a whale breached 30 yards away, and no one had seen it coming. This creature, the size of a house and with a tail the size of a room, came from just off the stern on the port side and the sound it made was the sound of the ocean throwing it at the sky, and I could not swear, even now, whether the predominant sound was one of moving water or moving air. Briefly, the whale towered, then it twisted so that its belly glowed white in the sun, and I thought: 'Moby Dick' (and Moby Dick was an albino humpback so it was of a humpback that Melville wrote, 'He is the most game-some and light-hearted of all the whales, making more gay foam and white water generally'), and it gate-crashed the ocean on its black back and the boat rocked. And the boat said, 'OOOOHHHHMMMMYYYYY-GAAAAAAHHHHDD!!!!!!'

They came round the boat then, at least four of them, and their proximity hushed the boat and commanded it to speak in whispers, which it did.

I was leaning over the gunwale and a humpback whale slid into place alongside, and it snorted from the blowhole that was not ten feet below me. I looked straight down into it, and the smell of its exhaled breath washed over my face. I cannot pretend that it was a pleasant smell, but I remember my response to it was to breathe out forcefully into it, and I can never forget that my breath and the breath of a wild humpback whale commingled. I wondered why a whale would come alongside the boat apparently inspecting what it found there, considering what men in boats had done to the species over the centuries, and I wondered if it picked up the positive energy that overflows the gunwales in any whale-watching boat, or if all whales are simply curious about all boats. Canadian nature writer Farley Mowat wrote in his 1972 book, *A Whale for the Killing,* of his old Uncle Art recalling childhood fishing trips off New-foundland when 'they was t'ousands of the big whales on the coast them times . . . Many's the toime a right girt bull, five times the length of our dory, would spout so close alongside you could have spit baccy down his vent. My old Dad claimed they'd do it a-purpose; a kind of joke you understand . . .'

Then the whale slid slowly forward and I was looking into its eye, and its eye, which was about four inches across, looked so blatantly, so directly at my eyes that I felt sought out, chosen, the subject of a predestined moment. Much later, back on land, I would raise the notion with a couple of fellow passengers. They had each felt exactly the same thing.

The skipper's voice:

'We are in among a pod of seven or eight hump-back whales. They're all around and below the boat. We're going to put a hydrophone over the side, and hopefully we'll hear them sing. So please stay quiet for a while.'

So the hydrophone had gone over the side. A tannoy speaker gurgled into life making underwater sounds and the boat filled up with gales of silence, and I waited to hear Ellingtonian jazz or Sibelius . . . then it began and it discarded at once my every preconceived musical reference point. It began like wolves, sliding from high to a mid-register note, but then it stopped abruptly, which is not the wolf's way. Then a second voice (I thought it was a second voice, but now I can't justify why), a squeak, higher and less tonally rounded than the first utterance, but also cut off abruptly, as though its function was percussive. Then a bass sound so low that it warbled uncertainly among the limits of any discernible notes. Oscar Peterson used that terrain on a piano keyboard that he had extended by several notes. They could be covered with a flap so that they didn't confuse other players unaccustomed to their presence. Their purpose was also percussive up to a point, but they also allowed him to cascade from known registers into unfamiliar depths. The new whale voice inhabited unfamiliar depths, but then rose as a second and then a third voice overlaid it, and suddenly I had restored to me the notion of Harry Carney's baritone underscoring the Ellington saxes. Then silence, water sounds.

Then something remarkably similar to what had gone before, remembered phrases. I am a part-time musician, but I have a full-time musician's ear that hears pitches and phrases in all manner of everyday sounds, and I bent my ear to what was going on. I looked for patterns. I became aware of a rhythm, profoundly slow, but more or less constant. Roger Payne, who made the scientific discovery that humpback whale voices were in fact songs in 1967, and who has studied them for 40 years, believes that ocean swells may determine the rhythm. Whales, he said, give the ocean its voice.

That voice has a range of seven octaves (exceptional human voices, like, say, Cleo Laine's, can encompass four octaves, my unexceptional voice can handle two and a bit), but like human singers, it moves among small intervals, and more remarkably, it also rhymes; the whale is also the ocean's poet. So I sat spellbound on a gently rocking boat in Glacier Bay, Alaska, listening to the ocean give voice.

Who taught you, Poet?
Who first caught your up-craning eye
and thought you fit to try out
a world-travelling song,
knowing your ways, bestowing
the pacific demeanour with which to navigate
between Alaska and the Tay?

And if I give you my most respectful silence,
my musician's ear and my writer's best endeavour,
can you reach me, teach me
themes and variations, cadence and nuance,

so that if I were to travel the earth
as you travel the girth of the ocean – singing –
I could be your tradition-bearer,
marry my voice to your singular song
and carry its worldly wisdom,
rhymes and all, to landlocked tribes
beyond the ocean's thrall?

One last dip into Roger Payne's exploration of hump-back songs (with one last grateful nod and unreserved endorsement of his exceptionally accomplished book, *Among Whales*): he acknowledges that their meaning remains a mystery ('They guard their secrets as effortlessly, as enigmatically as they always did'), as does their technique ('We don't even know where in their bodies to look for the sound-making apparatus. It seems reasonable to assume that humpbacks must use air to make sounds, yet they release no air while singing . . .') Perhaps they just hum.

Yet the whale song on the boat's tannoy in Glacier Bay did not sound like humming. Instead, as I started to tune in to what was going on, it reminded me again of wolves, not in the manner of the song's construction but something in the nature of its projection edged my ear that way. So I began to wonder in a fumbling, inexpert way if the whale song was at least in part a collective anthem in the same way wolves howl, advertising territory, location, strength, numbers, mood, asking and answering questions of the nearest pack, the nearest pod, or the nearest lone wanderers of the tribe. And lone wolves howl looking for other wolves, for company. The sound of a wolf pack's howl can travel five miles. In coastal packs, in places like Alaska, is it possible that wolves hear whales, and whales hear wolves? Given the much greater range of frequencies in the humpback's repertoire, and the capacity of oceans to transmit sound waves many times further than air, and the huge distances whales travel compared to wolves, it is reasonable to expect that their communication skills would be much more sophisticated. Yet as with wolves, the natural habitat of the humpback whale is travel. And as with whales, the wolf – whether in a pack or alone – travels its portion of the world singing.

Getting up close and very personal with wild whales has just this kind of effect on a susceptible human mind: the encounter compels you to engage with its mystery. This creature, so massive, so elementally beautiful, and so close that I could only engage with part of it at any one time, 'so close alongside you could have spit baccy down his vent', was at the same moment so untouchably distant and quite beyond comprehension. So you fall back on some facet of your own known world, relate it to that and see where that takes you, see what kind of light or understanding it might shed, bearing in mind that you start from the unhelpful position of a member of that species that set its face against nature in general and whales in particular a long time ago. It is not just biology that stands in the path of enlightenment.

The truly extraordinary aspect of that encounter with humpbacks was that the lasting enlightenment was shed not on the humpbacks by my own endeavours, but on my own place on the map – and therefore on me – by the humpbacks. It would take ten more years, but the witness I bore that day has illuminated in the most unimaginable way the events of 1883–84. It brought the Winter Whale back to life.

'Don't worry,' my host had told me. 'There will be other whales, and if you're lucky, they'll come to you.' It is my preferred way of working. I was lucky, again.

Chapter 16

Apologia

Go to the lee of the berg, wounded whale!
He welters in blood.
The eye dims, and the foundry heart is still.
George Mackay Brown
from 'Whale', 1986

I met the skeleton of the Tay Whale when I was about
five. I saw it sporadically through childhood, and I have
not seen it since, even though it is still there. Bits of dead
animals do nothing for me, even the intact skeleton of a
whale, which is arguably as impressive as bits of dead
animals get. Its impact on my childhood imagination
was wholly negative. I found it repulsive. It infiltrated
my dreams, which did nothing to endear it to me, for
I had many childhood dreams about wild animals
that lived and treated me well, and taught me not to
fear. The skeleton of the Tay Whale was a grotesque
counterweight to such dreams. It did nothing at all for
the cause of whales in my mind. I never learned, and
never asked, how the whale came to be there, nor what
kind of whale it was. As a young observer of a museum

exhibit I failed completely, or the exhibit failed me completely.

I became aware of McGonagall as a teenager, and because of his particular place in the affections of the city of my birth, I have been aware of him ever since, and I have read him haphazardly ever since, so I knew the poem. But it was a poem, not a historical document, and it was a McGonagall poem, so not to be taken seriously. It had nothing whatever to do with the wild world of whales. That began for me in the early summer of 1988, at the age of 40.

'You still there, Jim?'

'Uh-huh.'

'Come up and see this.'

'What is it?'

'Killer.'

That was the bait.

In the late summer of 1998 I met the humpbacks. That was the hook, line and sinker.

By then, of course, the politics of whaling and the conservation of whales were on the political agenda of every seafaring nation in the world, Greenpeace had been born and quickly evolved from a kind of provisional wing of whale conservation into mainstream thinking on the subject, whale-watching replaced whale-killing in the traditional whaling grounds of the world's oceans. And whenever, wherever in the world, the few remaining whaling nations went to work, the world's media followed and grew angry. The world's media couldn't get enough of whales, and it still can't. In that transformed climate, in 2006 a whale swam up the Thames as far as Tower Bridge and made the national news for days on end as rescuers tried to turn it back. Huge crowds gathered daily. Early in 2007 a small pod of killers swam up the Forth as far as the railway bridge and began to prey on a colony of grey seal pups. More headlines, newsreels, crowds and crowds, high on the allure of whales. Then, it got personal.

In the late summer of 2007, I was in the McManus Galleries and Museum in Dundee looking at paintings, and stumbled across a leaflet in the foyer. It simply said 'The Tay Whale' on the front, and there was a photograph of that skeleton. I flipped through it and put it in my pocket. I found it days later, and between the jacket pocket where I found it and the wastepaper basket where I intended to dump it, I read a few lines . . . 'In early December 1883, while Britain's largest whaling fleet wintered at home in Dundee, an unusual visitor swam along the shores of the Tay. The visitor was a male Humpback Whale, Megaptera novacngliae, a slow swimmer and an easy target for whalers . . .'

A humpback?

The Tay Whale was a *humpback*?

Two days later I was in the local history section of Dundee Central Library, where I asked what there might be in print about the Tay Whale. The answer, after a painstaking search, was nothing. Instead, they dug out a sheaf of photocopied newspaper reports from that winter of 1883–84, which I imagine I read with my mouth open and my head shaking in a state of mind-numbing disbelief. For I was reading, not about a museum exhibit, not about a strung-up assemblage of old bones, not about a creature that had been dead for 125 years, but about the most thrilling life-force my life has ever encountered. For by now humpback whales had 'propagated into the core of my very being' in Roger Payne's phrase; they had revealed themselves to me as 'the most gamesome and light-hearted of all whales', in Herman Melville's phrase; one had swum so close to me 'you could have spit baccy down his vent' in Uncle Art's phrase; and that same whale had looked so blatantly, so directly into my eyes that I felt sought out, chosen, the subject of a predestined moment. Suddenly the Tay Whale was a cause. I went looking for back-up and I found *Among Whales,* and in the writing of Roger Payne an ally of uncommon distinction.

An unhealthy cocktail of outrage and shame troubled that early research; the city and the river to which I belong had hosted a whale hunt and the citizens cheered the hunt to the echo. At every stage of the humiliation of the Tay Whale, they turned up in their thousands, this despite the fact that they saw what I saw in Glacier Bay, only more of it, and over six weeks. Why didn't the whale propagate into the very core of their being? Why didn't they become an infuriated mob, scupper the boats and tie up the whalers and howl down the hunt?

It is too easy to say that their attitude was a product of their time, that the city's prosperity was uniquely linked to the business of killing whales, that crowds routinely turned out every time the whalers left for the Arctic and every time they returned, cheering them off and cheering them home. There are two things wrong with that excuse. The first is that until the Tay Whale turned up, no one in the crowds other than the professional whalers themselves had seen a wild whale before, yet not even the humpback's characteristic demonstration of what a wild whale amounts to could change them. Oh, they gasped at every blow, and they clapped and cheered at every breaching, and they held their breath at every flourish of that room-sized tail, but then they cheered the coal sack on the flagpole that signified the first harpoon had struck home, and when Greasy Johnny got to work on the carcase they paid money to gawp at its wretchedness. And so, of course, in the climate of the times, did the people of Aberdeen, Glasgow, Manchester and Liverpool. The second flaw in that old excuse was that this was not a business transaction, this was a lynching.

Greasy Johnny made a circus freak show of a humpback whale and once I knew that the Tay Whale was a humpback, once I had discovered it could still have been cruising the oceans of the world, singing, I decided I would try and set the record straight. Because I have heard the humpback sing.

I imagine it's too late to apologise. American writer Barry Lopez tells in his short essay 'Apologia' of a man who challenged him for lifting road kills from the tarmac and giving them a softer last resting place in roadside grasses and woods. 'Once a man asked, Why do you bother? You never know, I said. The ones you give some semblance of burial, to whom you offer an apology, may have been like seers in a parallel culture. It is an act of respect, a technique of awareness.'

I like the notion, even if I am unpersuaded about the possibilities of a parallel culture. It may be, however, that if I had known all that I know now when I was in the company of the Glacier Bay humpbacks, when the four-inch eyeball glided past the hull of the boat directly below where I leaned out, and if I hadn't been in a boat that gasped aloud at every whale's every gesture, and if I hadn't been trying to make a radio programme at the time, and if . . . and if . . . and if . . . and if I had met that whale alone on a tranquil and empty sea, I would have tried to send him what I could. Perhaps I could have sung him something. Perhaps some wandering humpback will swim this way again, singing, and I will greet him from an empty shoreline stance, waving, and make my peace.

But what would I send him? After all, my home city is still rather proud of the Tay Whale, and even with the international pro-whale sensibility that prevails through much of the twenty-first-century world, the McGonagall connection still confers on its story something of the air of a merry jape. And anyway, my city is still inclined to ask as much of the world as cares to listen, who else has got a humpback whale skeleton in its cupboard and did you know it takes six men just to lift the skull? Dundee is no less proud of its whaling heritage, and that coupling of words provokes no embarrassment among those who brandish it as a badge of our achievements. I have a fundamental difficulty with the notion of whaling as heritage and I wince at the sight of the two words on the same page, never mind cheek-by-jowl in the same line of the same sentence. It was – it still is (and as I write this the Australians are haranguing the Japanese for their proposal to kill 1,000 humpbacks 'for scientific purposes') – the least forgivable of slaughters, sustained over centuries, achieving species extinctions and dooming other whale tribes to unsustainable population levels. And yes, I know that every nation that ever went whaling has its Dundee, and that most, like Dundee, have turned their backs on all that, and if a whale swam into the Tay today it would be marvelled at, admired and ushered back to the safety of the sea with heartfelt warmth. My birthplace has re-invented itself more than once, and has become a twenty-first-century city that operates at the cutting edge of medical science, notably in ground-breaking cancer research; that punches far above its weight in every endeavour of the arts. Yet it remains a place that cannot resist looking over its shoulder with a kind of nostalgic smirk to those days when its name was on the lips of the world. And when it was all over, the men and the ships and the shipbuilders effortlessly converted their unique accumulation of knowledge into the new and insatiable thirst for polar exploration, and Dundee became a worldwide by-word in that endeavour too.

Yet even if you allow all that, even if you are prepared to write it off as a product of its time (which is, I acknowledge, a mighty 'if'), or if not that at least allow that Dundee was no more culpable than anywhere else that sent ships to the whaling grounds, none of that excuses the killing of the Tay Whale. Nothing does.

I had a strange notion in Dundee one day. I was walking along the shore at Broughty Ferry, just because I love the place and it has been central to my life forever, and I thought it would assist the cause of this book if I went to see the skeleton again, armed with all the knowledge I had acquired in the 50 years that had elapsed since I last saw it. And if I went in a suitable frame of mind (although I was uncertain at that moment what 'suitable' might mean), perhaps something insightful would rub off in its presence. You never know. Perhaps it is still a seer in a parallel culture . . .

It didn't happen, because the museum was closed for major refurbishment and when I inquired about the possibility, I was told the skeleton was being stored in several pieces in several different local authority premises around the city. Did I know it took six men to lift the skull? Uh-huh.

So I'm left with the slim possibility that another humpback will stray into my home waters, to rub shoulders with the estuary's recently established population of dolphins and the recently reintroduced population of white-tailed eagles, and the biggest winter assembly of eider ducks in Europe; and where the Bell Rock Lighthouse still glitters like the lowest star in the huge night sky. It will surely know it has nothing to fear. After all, when the Thames whale died after days of round-the-clock rescue efforts, people in the crowds wept. The Forth killers ate their fill over a couple of weeks and disappeared, and those who had seen them kill seal cubs, of all endearingly photogenic creatures, responded, not swearing vengeance and brandishing words like 'savages', but with a collective 'that's-nature' shrug. Whales had come calling, and that was what mattered. They had felt chosen, the subject of a pre-destined moment.

And of course, the wandering humpback, being a world traveller, could easily have encountered – or received intelligence about – the humpback mother and calf that swam 75 miles upriver from San Francisco to Sacramento in May 2007. There they turned round, and started to make their way back to San Francisco, urged on every mile of the way by thousands and thousands of well-wishers. They made it all the way back to San Francisco Bay, too, but almost within sight of the Golden Gate Bridge they stopped, and California held its breath. The *San Francisco Chronicle* splashed the story on Wednesday, 30 May:

The two humpback whales that captured worldwide attention for their two-week sojourn in the Sacramento–San Joaquin River Delta returned to San Francisco Bay on Tuesday and came within only a few miles of the Golden Gate and their Pacific Ocean home.

By nightfall Tuesday, the mother and calf faced a swim of less than eight miles to the narrow channel under the Golden Gate Bridge – but they weren't leaving the bay just yet. Instead, the pair spent the early evening parading close to the Tiburon shore, delighting onlookers outfitted with binoculars. Then they appeared to settle for the night just off Larkspur.

It capped a day of significant progress for the whales, who had been exploring the delta since May 13. On Sunday they crossed under what seemed to be a major obstacle – the Rio Vista Bridge – and dawdled around the Benicia area until Tuesday morning. But around 10 a.m. they had darted under the Benicia and Carquinez bridges. They crossed under the Richmond–San Rafael Bridge and entered San Francisco Bay around 5 p.m. having travelled 30 miles.

Each time they sprinted several miles towards the ocean, they would periodically slow and frolic in the deep, salty water . . .

Exhausted scientists and government staffers grew increasingly excited Tuesday as they watched the whales head unaided toward the ocean. Several attempts last week to drive them from the delta with dissonant sounds and fire hoses were generally unsuccessful . . .

If the whales succeed in joining California–Mexico stock now feeding off the Farallon Islands, it's unclear if researchers will be able to chart the animals' progress. A telemetry tag that researchers had hoped to stick in the mother whale malfunctioned, thwarting attempts to track the whales by satellite. Efforts were under way Tuesday to obtain a replacement tag.

Large ships and ferries traversing San Francisco and San Pablo Bays seemed to take extra care to avoid the whales on Tuesday, said Coast Guard Lt. Cmdr. John Copley. The whales, which suffered large gashes after hitting a boat keel or propeller, were protected by the flotilla that enforced a 500-yard safety zone around the animals. The boats were to be called off overnight to protect both the crews and the whales.

If the humpbacks stay in San Francisco Bay, ferries could be re-routed today to avoid them. In such cases, ferry commuters could suffer delays, Copley said . . .

Apologia

Rod McInnis, the regional director of the fisheries department for the National Oceanic and Atmospheric Administration, said no cost estimates have been tallied on the rescue effort. But he rejected arguments that the whales were not worth the time and money spent so far.

'These aren't just any marine mammal – this is an endangered species,' McInnis said, noting that only around 1,200 humpbacks belonged to the California–Mexico population. 'This is a proven breeder and her young calf. They are worth saving.'

The cutting had been sent to me by an American friend, the New Hampshire-based painter Sherry Palmer. It had a hand written note on it: 'They are back at sea now!', accompanied by a drawing of a smiling face.

So a humpback whale turns up, and on a shore of the Tay estuary, I raised an arm in greeting.

Welcome whale.
What water is this?
The Tay estuary.
That means nothing. What ocean?
No ocean. The ocean lies back the way you have
  come, north then west, then the Atlantic.
This is a sad place.
Why? I am not sad. It is a beautiful place.

The Winter Whale

*You are not whale. It is a sad place for whales. The
waters tell me whales died here.*

*Many dead whales were brought here in ships. One
whale died here.*

Brought in ships by the killer men?

Yes.

What about the one that died here?

*He turned up alone, stayed to feed for six weeks. The
killer men were at home for the winter. They
belonged here. They went out in small boats for
him and he died slowly.*

Do you belong here too?

Yes.

Yet you are a friend of whales?

*Yes. We are all friends of whales now. We have
changed. You have nothing to fear here. The whale
that died is a bitter inheritance for me.*

I can feel him. He is still here.

His bones are here.

His bones are still here? I can feel him. He is still here.

*Yes. I regret the death. I regret that the bones are still
here.*

*You must not keep him. Where the bones are is not a
whale place.*

No, it is not a whale place. It has walls and a roof.

The whale must not live within walls or under a roof.

He does not live. He was killed 125 years ago.

The whale must not live within walls or under a roof.

Apologia

Do you think he still lives on through the bones?
You say you have changed in the last 125 years but you
 do not know that the whale lives on in the bones.
 The whale must not live within walls or under a roof.
Where then?
Where he belongs, as you live where you belong.
Where does the whale belong?
He belongs where he last swam, where the lowest star
 in the sky beckons.
Do you want the bones returned to the sea?
It is not the bones you must return, it is the whale.
Will that appease . . .?
Yes! That will dispel the sadness of whales in this
 water where you belong. It will also be better for
 you with the sadness gone.
Yes, I would like your sadness to be gone from these
 waters.
Then will you see to it? Will you see to it that the
 whale is returned to the place where he belongs?
I will do what I can, yes.
See to it. Tell me you will see to it.
Yes. I will see to it.
Now, tell me about the whales that were brought back
 dead in the ships. What did the killer men do with
 them?
We made a fabric – like a skin – called jute. Whale oil
 made it work for us.
What did you use it for?

The Winter Whale

*To make the sails of ships so that we could travel the
oceans of the world, to make the ropes and rigging
for ships, to cover the wagons of travellers who
crossed all that land between the Atlantic and the
Pacific. Whales helped us to be world travellers.
Whales understand world travellers. It was overdone,
the whale killing, but whales understand world
travellers. Whales travel the world and also kill as
they travel. But it was overdone, the whale killing.
Yes.
Put my Brother Whale back where he belongs, then
you will have made your peace.*

The whale lifted one long flipper and held it aloft,
waving gently. It was the last I saw of him as he went
under. I stayed out there on the edge of the ebb-tide
watching the sea through the late afternoon into the
dusk, until the first light glittered suddenly from the
lowest star in the whale's sky.

Bibliography

Bullen, Frank T., *The Cruise of the Cachalot Round the World after Sperm Whales* (1898)

Gifford, Professor Douglas, *The History of Scottish Literature* (Aberdeen University Press, 1989)

Jones, David, *Whales* (Whitecap, 1998)

Konrad of Megenberg, *Das Buch der Natur* (1475)

Lopez, Barry, *Apologia* (University of Georgia, 1998) and *Of Wolves and Men* (Touchstone, 1978)

Maxwell, Gavin, *Ring of Bright Water* (Allen Lane, 1960)

Melville, Herman, *Moby Dick* (1851)

Mowat, Farley, *A Whale for the Killing* (McLelland and Stewart, 1972)

Payne, Roger, *Among Whales* (Scribner, 1998)

Scoresby, William, *An Account of the Arctic Regions with a Description of the Northern Whale Fishery* (1820)

Watson, Lyall and Ritchie, Tom, *Whales of the World* (Hutchinson, 1981)

Watson, Norman, *The Dundee Whalers* (Tuckwell, 2003)

Williams, Heathcote, *Whale Nation* (Cape, 1988)

Wittig, Kurt, *The Scottish Tradition in Literature* (Oliver & Boyd, 1958)